MW01703040

STEVE BILSBOROUGH

JUDAH RISE

"AND THE LORD SAID, JUDAH SHALL GO UP FIRST"
JUDGES 20:18

Published by Steve Bilsborough Ministries
14494 Cortez Blvd.
Spring Hill, Florida 14494

ISBN: 979-8-9874436-1-3 (Paperback)

Cover Artist & Design by: Jordan Douglas | Goldin Productions
Copy and Editing by: Meriem McLaughlin | Domenica Motacek

For Additional Copies or Inquiries:
Steve Bilsborough Ministries
www.stevebilsborough.com

First Print Edition - February 2023

I dedicate this book to my incredible wife, Ellen,

who makes each day a great day.

PREFACE

It seems like we have come through so much in the past several years, both in the world and in the church. Although some may feel like they have never seen anything quite like the life-altering events of our recent past, history records a much more detailed account of the challenges man has had to face since the beginning of time. The fight for survival is real, and though it may often seem unrelated to most of our lives, there are men and women who, over time, have had to go to extreme measures to hold onto what we have today.

Our freedom and liberties are worth fighting for, and even worth dying for. Today we are blessed to be able to live in a world, in which we get to embrace our families, our loved ones, and especially God, even amidst some of the ongoing conflicts that beset us.

Why "Judah Rise?" First, because there is a necessity for the Church to keep focused on the purpose for its existence. As Christians, our very reason for being is to bring people to Jesus Christ and any deviation from this would hurt the cause. And second, because there is fragmentation. Like a woven tapestry that, after many years of use, begins to show its wear, with unraveling threads and tears in the fabric, the true picture of the Church and its splendor has now digressed into a semblance of what it once was. Yet things are not always as they appear, because underneath the worn fabric, the faded facade and the weary faces still lies this great and powerful institution Jesus died for, His Church!

It is my prayer that “Judah Rise” will reignite the fire that once burned in the hearts of preachers, pastors, and believers everywhere. ***Let Judah Rise!***

FORWARD

A fervent, endless, and compelling desire to share the Gospel to every ear that will hear. People always ask what my husband is all about. Is he for real? I can think of no greater way to describe his heartbeat than this statement. He is about souls and has always been about souls. It has been his top priority since his youth, when he began preaching at the young age of 15 and led over 300 youth kids to the Lord. In his early college years, through evangelism and mission trips to over 37 nations around the world, he has seen miracle after miracle. I have watched him build churches, cast vision, lead, mentor, and inspire everyone around him to be greater and always aspire for more.

I am so excited about this book more than any other book I've read. I am blessed to have walked this journey alongside my husband for over 32 years. This isn't just a book for the sake of writing another book. There are many good books out there. This is a divine download from Heaven at the leading of the Holy Spirit. What is inside of you will come out of you. Judah Rise wasn't just a theme for 2022 in our ministry. It was a forever declaration stating that the true believer cannot be silenced or lie dormant. We must rise like a mighty remnant army, standing together stronger than ever. Judah is first. On the front lines of battle. Not whimpering in the back row. Now is not the time to live lukewarm and be passive. We are not ashamed of the gospel. We proudly proclaim Judah Rise.

My Stephen is the greatest example I know of a man who walks with God. He hears from God and will not move without His leading. I am so honored and blessed to do life with him. As you read this book, I know that you will be blessed. My prayer is that you will allow "Judah Rise" to live inside of you. Each one of us has an assignment. Reading this book will equip you and I for greater things ahead and put us in our rightful place to fulfill the Father's will in all that we do for His glory in the Kingdom.

Inspire Others for the Kingdom!
Pastor Ellen Bilsborough

CONTENTS

INTRODUCTION

Allow me to set the stage if you will. There, in a place called Mizpah, are gathered all the men of Israel, standing together as one. Every tribe was represented, from Dan to Beersheba. An intimidating force to say the least, it included 400 divisions of expert swordsmen. This was certainly no family reunion, but it was family.

A tragedy had taken place, a woman had died as a result of the savage abuse by the men of Gibeah, from a Benjamite town. A Levite who was the husband of this murdered woman demanded Israel take action. The response was more than reasonable, let us find the men who are guilty of this vile crime and make them pay for what they had done, but the Benjamites would not allow such a thing to happen.

Rather than surrendering the guilty men, they chose rather to go against their own family and fight. Thus, the battle begins, and herein lies the story of this tragic family against family battle.

Blood was shed, lives were lost, and it might even be said that no real winner was declared; yet in the end, Israel prevailed.

Much of Israel's history is a story for us to read today, a learning curve of true to life experiences we must learn from, that describes in detail some of the most horrific battles, mixed with choices that often broke the heart of God. Idolatry, immorality, and impurity were just a few of the unwise choices these people of God made, yet over and over again, God came to them to bring them out of the very things they had gotten themselves into.

Their only hope not only in this great battle, but in all their battles, was God, and the patterns He had set before them. Proverbs 14:34 tells us ***"Righteousness exalteth a nation, but sin is a reproach to any people."***

When Judah is first, victory is assured! Their question was right, but their heart was still not where it should have been. "Who should we send God?" was their question, and God gave the answer; yet victory evaded them. Why?

In Matthew 15:8, Jesus himself refers to a people that honor God with their lips, but their heart is far from Him. Judah must go first, but God must come first.

We are closer each day to the coming of the Lord and live our lives with the hope of His soon return, but until that day, we fight this battle of faith, dressed and ready for the daily confrontation with the enemy and the ever-present conflict, for the destiny of mankind.

Send Judah First!

CHAPTER ONE

Is There Not A Cause?

And David said, What have I now done?
Is there not a cause?

I Samuel 17:29

There is a razor thin line that hangs in the balance between the desire for peace among men versus the need to stand up for a cause. General William Tecumseh Sherman, in the Civil War era, wrote in his shortened version to the city officials in Atlanta that, "War Is Hell." Nobody truly desires to see the travesty of war, the bloodshed, the loss of life, or the devastation to nations; yet it has always been an often-unavoidable reality in our world. Regardless of the reasons for it, conflict has existed since the time of Adam. It can come in the form of brotherly jealousy, such as when Cain's envy of his brother fueled a rage within him that prompted him to murder Abel. It can also stem from territorial disputes, from lust for position and power, or even from the religious discord that is so prevalent in many countries in the modern world.

There is a very real enemy, whose sole purpose is to steal all that God has created and destroy it, with mankind being at the top of the list. He seeks out the vulnerable and ill-equipped, the weakened of the herd, so to speak, as his prey. His strategy is to lull mankind into the deceptive illusion of comfort and bliss and to remind us that when we live in peace God is pleased, and He is; but the devil manipulates God's Word in an attempt to trick us into thinking we are at peace, when we are, in fact, engaged in the greatest war of all time, with eternal implications for the souls of mankind. In peace, we can find ourselves often unprepared, caught off guard, and certainly not ready for battle, thus allowing him to prey on the untrained and ill-prepared.

The reality is this, there is no "second place" in war! You are either first or you are dead! The luxury of passivity is not afforded to the Christian. When lives and eternity lie in the balance, there is too much at stake. If you want to win, you have to fight; and if you are to fight, then you must prepare for the battle. This Latin quote encapsulates the essence of this book. It simply says, "is vis pacer para vellum." Translated, it means "If you want peace, prepare for war."

The cause is what compels men to act, to respond and, if necessary, to fight for what is right, moral, and vital to our survival. I am personally unaware of any historical era that was completely void of any worthy causes. Throughout history, men have fought in some of the bloodiest battles, leaving behind their families, risking all of their worldly possessions, and even giving up their lives for causes they considered vitally important. We have fought for land, for religion, for freedom, for liberty, for justice, for politics and for many other justified and unjustified reasons; and right or wrong, in their minds, the causes must have been significant enough to elicit a reaction.

I suppose that the question that comes before us, when we have to consider the present and the future of the world today, is, "Is there not a cause?" One of the more recent wars in my lifetime, "Operation Desert Storm," occurred in the early 1990's, when the larger country of Iraq invaded the smaller nation of Kuwait. This unjustified attack incited a response from an even larger country, the United States, who, along with its allies, purposed to drive out the invader. Certainly, there was a whole lot more to it than this simple depiction, but for brevity, we will just say this is what it was. An invader! Nothing is more intrusive than someone having the audacity to access what does not belong to them, thus striking fear in people and, more often than not, invoking a response. Generally, attempts at peaceful negotiations with an invader are nothing short of futile, and force becomes the only recourse to combat their obtrusive actions and expel them from where they do not belong.

Today, in America, there is an invasion in process! It is interesting to observe, as it is happening right before our very eyes. When an aggressor plans his attack, he often does it with subtlety in mind, with a slow seduction, much like a predatory animal sneaking up on its prey. Once invaders become convinced that they have reached a domineering position, where they cannot be opposed, they become more aggressive and forceful.

Even the most notorious dictators did not start out with the brutality that we read about in history books. It is even possible that they set out with good intentions that went terribly bad over time.

Today, and historically in Christendom, many have started out in the Spirit only to end up in the flesh. Good men, even some in ministry, who once held high the banner of the Cross, declaring righteousness and holiness, have been deceived by the seduction of fame, money, power, and position. I have lived long enough to see the shattered pieces of their lives fade into obscurity, often leaving a trail of devastated followers, confused as to how and why this could have happened.

Every person who has ever suffered injury or death fighting a justified battle for a cause they believed in deserves to be honored and esteemed. There is no question that these great heroes, both past and present, deserve to be memorialized. But it is important to understand that there is no battle that has ever been fought whose importance surpasses the greatest cause of all, the fight for man's soul, for eternal liberty and for freedom. This is the cause we fight for, and this is why a fresh revelation of the principle of "first" is so important, because it is only when Judah goes first that victory is assured.

It is for this reason, that I believe God is calling us, sending a clear message to His Church, calling up the ranks, summoning

His people like never before to hear the sound of the bugle calling us to war. There is an invasion the likes of which we have never seen before. The wickedness of man has always been great, but could it ever have equaled what we are seeing today? Noah knew the depths of depravity; he saw it before his very eyes, the wickedness of man. He lived in the very atmosphere of barbarism, among wicked and perverse minds taken over by a seducing spirit. Surely, he must have asked himself if it could ever get worse than this. What more could man's mind think of to do to go against the nature of God? How far could man fall into the abyss of hedonism?

Why would God use this very period of time in Biblical history to remind us in Matthew Chapter 24:37 that, ***"As it was in the days of Noah, so shall also the coming of the Son of Man be."*** Did God know that conflict would mark every day of man's life until, and only until, the Prince of Peace makes His appearance to settle all debts?

I shudder to think of what it must have been like during the time of Lot, when perversion permeated the very fabric of society. How far could man possibly go until someone would stand up and say, "Enough is enough?" What depth of sin would it take to sound the alarm?

The answer is, the alarm has sounded; in fact, a long time ago, that crystal clear, atmosphere piercing blast came forth, "Let Judah Rise."

Through the Bible and history, itself, to do a comparative analysis on the moral failure of mankind, when it comes to the sins of the past and the sins of today would be difficult to say the least. Could it be possible that it was as wicked in Noah's day as it is today? Because that is what the Bible says. Is it possible that God came to a place even in New Testament history that He was ready to willingly turn man over to his reprobate mind? Let's not forget that the writer in Romans Chapter One was referring to men who once knew God but had since exchanged the truth of God for a lie.

There is no need to try to authenticate or justify the cause. It is very real and very much alive today. And contrary to what some more pacifistic people may feel, a more aggressive response is required, if we are to rescue as many people as possible from the eternal separation from God known as hell.

The well-known city of Jericho required an aggressive response. One might argue that no weapon was ever drawn, but that would not be true. In fact, this is where we begin to see the unfolding of the strategy for a winning Church: A mighty army of God coming to life and springing into action. The weapons that were drawn and the warfare that ensued most certainly took place, but it looked quite different from what the world's conception of war is. Paul said in Ephesians Chapter Six, ***"Finally, my brethren, be strong in the Lord, and in the power of His might. Put on the whole armor of God, that ye may be able to stand against the wiles of the devil. For we wrestle not against flesh and blood, but against principalities, against powers, against the rulers of the darkness of this world, against spiritual wickedness in high places."***

If you want peace, you need an army, trained, prepared and ready to, if necessary, lay down their lives for the protection of its citizens from every foe, near and far. The Prophet Amos reminds us, ***"Woe to you who are at ease in Zion."*** (Amos 6:1)

The New Living Translation says it like this, ***"What sorrow awaits you who lounge in luxury in Jerusalem, and you who feel secure in Samaria!"*** What a sobering call to all who call Jesus our Lord and Savior, that we must be ready at all times, trained, and on guard, for the adversary comes as a roaring lion, seeking whom he may devour.

What about Jericho? During those arduous days of walking in obedience, day after day for six days, quietly holding their breath, the Israelites were sure that God knew something that they did not. Throughout each day, the formidable walls silently mocked the Israelites, as they marched around the outer circumference of Jericho. Imagine not knowing how, but just knowing that somehow, God was going to remove this obstacle that blocked their access into His great promise, a land that flowed with milk and honey. Why this way? What was God's plan that required them to walk, once every day for six days, and now seven times on the seventh day? What could God possibly be thinking in this exhaustive approach to what Joshua called "victory?"

Judah has a way of showing up in almost every situation. At the church that I pastor, the word, "Judah " has become one that rolls off the tips of our tongues, when it comes to fighting spiritual battles. "Judah" is available to all believers, but because many either do not know or do not understand the secret of its power, it is not always accessed. Invaders are mortified when they see Judah show up. Aggressors are neutralized when they see Judah show up. In fact, part of hell's strategy is to keep God's people away from the knowledge of the power that is available to them, if they ever really knew Judah, our praise. Yes, trumpets were blown, rams horns declared the sound of victory, the shout of the people must have been heard for miles away; but what brought the walls down was not what some of the brilliant yet secular minds of our society, now and times past, have thought it to be. It was not a seismic event, nor was it a structural failure. Imagine walls so impenetrable, collapsing because people walked around them. I think not! What brought Jericho's walls down was a people united in obedience, trusting God who incited the power of praise into their situation. Whenever you lift a shout to God, you send shock waves through hell. I have no doubt that hell needed a clean-up crew that day, just to put everything back in order. The walls came down as promised by God, opening the gateway to the Promised Land, where provision would now be available, and God's people would prevail.

“Judah Rise” is more than just a manuscript put into print form and called a book. It is a call to every mighty warrior and those who desire to be. It is a splash of cold water in the face of every saint to recognize this reality and commit to do something about it before it is too late.

These great stories of bravery and courage offer us hope, stir our faith, and even inspire us. Yet with all of our historical evidence of great victories of the past, they cannot win our battles for us today; but rather, we must each stand on our own faith, and understand our own ability to draw on the strength of the Judah that rests in each of us who believe.

Is there not a cause? David’s words are more alive to us today than ever before. With absolute certainty, we must agree; the cause is great, but we are not alone. We are equipped with weapons that our adversary cannot understand; therefore, we have the capability to defeat him.

Although we see little of America in end-time Bible prophecy, we do see America today as the great influencer of the world for God. It has been said, "As America goes, so goes the world," So we have this moment, this time in our history, to change our world and to make a global impact in the limited time we have from this great land. ***"Let Judah Rise."***

CHAPTER TWO

Our God Whom We Serve Is Able!

If it be so, our God whom we serve is able to deliver us from the burning fiery furnace, and He will deliver us out of thine hand, O king. But if not, be it known unto thee, O king, that we will not serve thy gods, nor worship the golden image which thou hast set up.

Danial 3:17 & 18

It was early 2019 and, as I do every year, I was preparing, praying and seeking God for His direction for our ministry theme for the coming year of 2020. Although I am not an advocate of catch phrases and cute words that rhyme to launch into a new year, I do believe that people catch the heart of a thing when you attach a theme to it. Little did we know that the year that was ahead of us was to be one that would grip the entire planet. No one knew; it came upon the world like an undetected left hook to the jaw, like a southpaw catching its opponent off-guard, and no one was ready to deal with it. In fact, it was already here in America. It is just that America did not know what it was, had no name for it, and most definitely was not prepared for what was to come.

It came to me to set the course and direction of our year with the theme "All Things New." It was not too many days after we had launched into 2020, that the reality of those words became like a branding iron on our hearts and souls. I would have thought that what I felt God had given me was to bring us into this new year with such a celebration of what was to come, an excitement, an energy and an anticipation for what God was about to do in us, His Church, and even in the world.

There is always that expectancy, when coming into a new year, of better things to come, putting the past behind us and embracing what is yet unknown, and excitedly lunging forward into it. We all, with few exceptions, hoped for greater things ahead. What a shock it was to watch the news and hear the stories of so many people falling ill to something we had never encountered before. I cannot say for sure statistically, but I would presume that there is not a person in America, and possibly around the world, who did not know of someone who was affected by what we came to call COVID.

Was it a manufactured virus that escaped from a laboratory in Wuhan, China? Was it a mistake, a mishap that got out of control? Did anyone know anything ahead of time? Even still, there are so many questions that remain unanswered. What we do know for sure is there are few things that have brought a greater divide to humanity than what took place in 2020. Truly, it was a year of "All Things New," because this certainly was new to all of us.

I must admit that it was not what I imagined, when I launched that theme for the year in our ministry; in fact, it was the furthest thing from my mind. What I was expecting for the year and what actually took place were as far as the East is from the West, as far as I was concerned. I watched a strong, healthy man in our ministry fight for his life and eventually lose the battle to something that still had no name. I watched families weep in hospital corridors, makeshift morgues being constructed from tractor trailers, doctors shaking their heads in disbelief, and nurses running on pure adrenaline trying to assist those who could not find breath in their lungs. It was serious, and it was tragic.

As real as the pandemic was, the fear that surrounded it was every bit as real. I was getting calls in my office from people I loved and respected, talking about military invasions, the end of the world events getting ready to take place, hostile takeovers of America. I mean, it was absolutely mind-blowing to hear such apocalyptic conversations taking place from people who would normally be considered well-balanced, sound-minded people.

By far, what was most troubling about this entire season of sadness was that the world had no opportunity to be proactive. No prophet in the land was forecasting what was to come; no preacher was heralding the message of imminent urgency. There was no warning, no time for preparation, nothing. Presidents were perplexed, politicians were puzzled, people were paranoid, and humanity was now faced with a global issue, with no time to prepare beforehand.

The loss of life is never acceptable, and these deaths caused unbearable grief to so many people. But in many ways, this event was so much more than just that. This was not the first plague ever to happen in history, nor will it be the last. Man has been here before. We have an innate ability to recover and rebuild, and we have in many ways already done so. This year of horrific confusion, sickness and death will not soon be forgotten. It will forever be written in the history books for generations to read, should the Lord's return not take place first.

The word "new" in my theme for the year 2020 meant to me something exciting, and yet, it appeared that nothing exciting was to come of this entire year. The news grew worse each day. The entire global system shifted from anticipation to agony; expectancy made a 180 degree turn and went from the highest levels of optimism to the lowest levels of despair.
We survived once again, and outside of the political division of our nation, we seem to be rising again.

Or did we? I promise, or will do my best at least, to let this opening chapter be my only reflection on the events of 2020;

but this contemplation is vital, if we are to find the benchmark on which to rebuild. The World Trade Center towers have been replaced by a brand new, architecturally beautiful tower we call the “Freedom Tower.” It stands 1776 feet above the earth's surface and is symbolic of the year of the signing of the “Declaration of Independence” here in the United States of America. It is the evidence of man's ability to rise above the heaps of destruction left behind by demon-crazed assassins and once again restore hope into the hearts of Americans and people around the world.

It reflects strength, unity, and a future for mankind; but even still, it is temporal. What took place over the past several years in the natural, as tragic as it was, still pales in comparison to the greater issues facing the world today. Man’s greatest need is not longevity, health, and wealth. From the moment we are born, we begin the process of death. Deterioration is in constant motion in our physical bodies, and as much as we work to put it off, it is inevitable. Death is an enemy, and some have met this enemy prematurely, while others have lived long and fulfilled lives. But equally, we are all on course for an appointment that will never be canceled.

One of my favorite pastimes has been to build, not as a finished carpenter, as I do not have the patience for that, but as a visionary framer. I see it, draw it and build it. Over the years, I have built churches, houses, yes even bird houses. Several years ago, I was building our family a new home. I had probably gone bigger than I should have, but when you draw the plan out on a napkin in a coffee shop, the final result is not readily seen until construction begins, and you look at the blueprint and ask, "What have I done?"

This was a large home, bigger than intended, but we were too far into it to turn back, so we kept going. What I found quite amazing during this project, throughout the pouring of the footers, the twelve-inch foundation blocks, the poured concrete floors and all that we were doing, was that the two Italian block and brick layer gentlemen I had been working with based the entire structure on one nail. We were building on seven acres of land, with hundreds of pine trees, and I distinctly remember, throughout the entire project, seeing one tree with a small circle painted with fluorescent spray paint, with a nail in the middle of the circle. They called it "their benchmark." From the very beginning of the project, which incorporated the footers, it was this little nail that became the benchmark for everything.

I said to them one day, "Are you not concerned that, over the course of the next six months or so, the tree will grow, and the nail will move making all your levels inaccurate?" I will never forget their response: "The nail will never move." I was intrigued to learn that even if the tree grew another 20 feet, that nail would stay in its exact current location.

In the story of Shadrach, Meschach and Abednego, there was a decree in the land, during a time when idol worship was very prevalent. The decree sent forth was simple, when the music plays, everyone must bow down to worship the god of Nebuchadnezzar. This 90-foot tall, nine foot wide statue towered over the land, symbolizing, yet again, another false god that the people were required to worship. The Bible does not give all the details, but it does tell us that anyone who refused to bow down at the appointed time would be put into a fiery furnace. People bowed, not just because they truly believed in the idol the king had built, but because they feared the furnace. Great leaders never bow to fear. They rise up to face the adversary that stands in front of them. True leaders say things like ***"If it be so, our God whom we serve is able to deliver us from the burning fiery furnace, and He will deliver us out of thine hand, O king. But if not, be it known unto thee, O king, that we will not serve thy gods, nor worship the golden image which thou hast set up."*** (Daniel 3:17).

You cannot help but be inspired by the heroic stance of these three Hebrews. It is estimated that each of them was somewhere between the ages of fifteen and twenty years of age; and yet, even as young as they were, they had already made a decision not to allow fear of the furnace to cause them to compromise their calling.

Their faith in God was so much greater than the fear they had of the reprisal. They loved their lives even unto death, and for that reason, death cannot be seen as the aspiration of our lives to avoid, but rather as the door to all that God has prepared for us. These young men were sure that their God would be with them, but even if they did not survive the furnace, they were confident that eternity was so much greater than the temporal.

What did these young men have that so many lack today? It certainly is a wake-up call, to the "Spiritually Elite," that age and maturity and education and degrees do not necessarily qualify us to win the battle in the arena of faith. What gave them such assurance that they did not need to be afraid, even if they heated the fire seven times hotter? Could it be that they had something that many Christians fell short of during the past several years, in a time of testing, when the fear of COVID was piercing hearts in pews and pulpits, bookstores and banks, coffee shops and confectioneries? Is it possible that the Church was ill-prepared and got caught off guard? Could it be that some partook of the same toxic tonic that left Rip Van Winkle asleep for twenty years, only to wake and find himself in a very different world?

Has the Church been shipwrecked on the shores of the land of Lilliput, only to be tied up by those much less powerful than us? Have the Gulliver's of God become the gullible of God and allowed the enemy to paralyze them with a spirit of fear? What was it that enabled these three teenage boys to have the faith to make such bold statements? Could it be that they had come to know of a God that never moves, the one that

Malachi the Prophet said, ***"I am the LORD, I change not,"*** the one James described by saying that in Him there is no variableness, neither shadow of turning? Greater still is the writer of Hebrews who reminds us that He is the same, yesterday, today and forever. God will never be less than He is right now, nor will He ever be less than He was to these three Hebrew boys. As He revealed Himself in the past, He is the same in the present and future. So, what caused them to have such faith and confidence in God? It could only be that they knew Him as the unmovable, unshakable God in the same way my bricklayers knew that the nail they placed in a tree would never move regardless of how much time passed by.

We lived in the home that we built for about three years. One day, I was walking in the back forest on the property, still decorated with hundreds of pine trees. The wind was blowing through those trees, and they danced in the wind, swaying and bending back and forth, causing me to wonder if they might just break at some point. I looked up to see the pine needles falling, the trees swaying and the wind whistling, and then I looked down. It had been a few years now, but there, to my amazement, was a faded fluorescent circle on the bottom of one of the trees. The snow had come and gone for several years. The rain had fallen; the leaves had piled up; the pine needles had gathered on the ground; yet as I looked at the circle, in the middle of it, the same nail that had been placed in that tree nearly four years prior had remained intact.

It had not moved, the tree had grown, the trunk of the tree was larger, everything else had changed, but the nail remained the same. God is just like that nail, as strong and powerful as ever. He never moved, but we did. The Church was not ready! We had moved, moved from great faith to shallow faith, moved from a powerful mighty army to a paralyzed position of fear. We moved, over a period of time, and at an opportune time, the enemy came, and though weaker, smaller and less powerful, he capitalized on our fear and caught us in a place of vulnerability.

As we were coming to the end of 2020, I felt the Lord say, call this next year "Take Dominion." And that became our theme for the first year post-COVID. It was not until later in 2021, once again sitting in my place of study, that God said now, ***"Let Judah Rise."***

CHAPTER THREE

There Is A Sound!

Go up now, look toward the sea. And he went up, and looked, and said, There is nothing. And he said, Go again seven times.

I Kings 18:43

There is, without a doubt, nothing that can satisfy true thirst like water. The Psalmist said in Psalm 63:1, ***"Oh God, You are my God, early will I seek You, my soul thirsts for You."*** The Prophet Joel referenced this when he spoke of an outpouring so great, that even our sons and daughters would prophesy, our old men would dream dreams and our young men would see visions. Like a child incessantly asking, "Are we there yet?" from the back seat, during a long car ride, so too is the remnant Church crying out for the rain of Heaven to fall upon thirsty souls. The hearts of the hungry are yearning for this scripture to be fulfilled, not just for the outpouring, but also because this will be what ushers in the coming of the Lord. This great promise of God only takes place in the last days. We need the rain of Heaven to fall upon our land one more time. As those who have blazed trails of righteousness in recent history are being called home to their heavenly rewards, let the ones who follow pick up the mantle like an Elijah to Elisha, and use it to usher in the greatest last days outpouring ever seen.

We are inundated with organized religion here in America. The landscape is dotted with churches of every imaginable denomination on almost every corner, and yet still, there is so much more God has for us. Despite the many ways the gospel is being spread, through social media, Christian television, Bible printings, literature distribution, and massive crusades, we still fall so short of what is actually needed in the hearts of men and women today. Our choreographed services, with the special effects of a Broadway production, mesmerize people temporarily, but they produce very few long term results.

Many of our Sunday morning services are powerless presentations of a God that was, but not a God that is. What would we do without our iPads, LED screens, laser lights and smoke machines? The worst nightmare for some preachers would be to have a blackout during a service, forcing them to actually have to minister without the aid of all the devices we have embraced. When will we learn that people today are no longer satisfied with structured, choreographed, and predictable gatherings? They want rain! American clergy have increasingly hosted ecumenical events that seem to be on the rise in American churches, heralding the message of unity, while their hearts are far from pure, and their motives are far from holy. Rain has a cleansing effect; it purges and purifies, washes, and renews. When rain falls, hope comes, and joy is restored.

I believe that God has grown weary of empty, lifeless services, where He is denied the opportunity to display His glory and to reveal His power. We have come to understand, in recent years, exactly what Luke described in the 18th chapter, ***"When the Son of Man returns, will He find faith on the earth?"*** (v. 8). A preacher with no prayer life will have no passion, and a passionless preacher will inevitably have an anesthetizing effect upon his congregation, which does little to advance the Kingdom. I do not fault all preachers, but some must take ownership of the spiritual condition of those they lead. The

Bible is very explicit that those who teach will be held to a higher standard. When America was held hostage by a pandemic, we understood the fear in the hearts of men who did not know God; but there was no excuse for a fear so intense in the hearts of our spiritual leaders that it prompted them to close the doors to their churches. Some called it wisdom; some used the analogy of caring for their brothers; and others just flat out buckled at the knees and walked away from their pulpits altogether.

Faith never looks back, but neither does it look around. Rather than looking up to Jesus, entirely too many preachers looked to the left or to the right. At a time when the world needed to see a demonstration of God's power, many failed the test and took the path of least resistance. Some turned on one another and even went so far as to turn one another in to the authorities. Pastors were fined and imprisoned, only to be labeled as an embarrassment in their own churches, even by their own colleagues. Yes, we are a little down the road from that time now, but history has a way of repeating itself. As time passes and memory fades, history has repeatedly proven that events from the past can cycle back to become our present reality. Yet we should not fear what is to come, but rather, we should be looking for He who is to come with great anticipation and expectation.

If we are truly to take this nation and the world back for God in these last days, our Sunday morning services should look like a Holy Ghost hurricane swept through them. When were the altars last filled to overflowing with people weeping before the Lord? I do not say this to boast, but there is not a Sunday that goes by in our church that ten, fifteen, twenty or even more people come to know Jesus Christ. And although that might seem like a small number to some, it is important to remember that the angels rejoice over just one repentant sinner turning to Jesus.

Many of our more modern churches have not even made room for altars, as their front row seats are a knee's distance from the platforms. Salvations are now done by QR codes and church apps, while healing lines, miracles and deliverances have been discarded as a thing of the past. If we are not careful, what was once the norm in Pentecost will now be labeled as extreme, ostracizing those who preach for miracles as out of touch with the modern day church.

Have we become so consumed with our presentation that we have omitted the very thing we need the most? Where are the "rainmakers?" Yes, there has been a drought far greater than most realize or care to admit, but there is hope. God is raising up Elijahs who know the posture of prayer, men and women, young and old, who will not fold at the first attempt to stop them, because they know in their hearts that what God has promised, He will also perform. It was a question that God asked, not a statement, "Will He find faith?" and for that I am so thankful, because it leaves us in a place of decision. We hold the keys to breakthrough and revival. God's supernatural power has always been available, but it has never been automatic; it requires something of us. Psalm 67:5-6 tells us to ***"Let the people praise Thee, O God; Let all the people praise Thee. Then shall the earth yield her increase: and God, even our own God, shall bless us."***

Could it be that we have entered the era of the erosion of faith? Are we seeing Luke's words come to pass before the very eyes of this generation? We need to be reminded that faith is the very foundation upon which the Christian Church stands. We have nothing if we do not have faith. The writer of Hebrews reminds us time and again of this non-negotiable element that must be the primary characteristic in our walk with God. It took faith for Elijah to believe for rain, not just with his words, but also with his actions. God uses the number seven 735 times in the Bible. Seven is a number that speaks of completeness or perfection. It is, in fact, the symbol of God's authority and power over all things on the earth. Seven times, Elijah's servant had to go and see, until what he saw was enough to prove that God was, in fact, getting ready to send the rain.

Was it a cloud the size of a man's hand that convinced Elijah that God was about to send the rain? Not at all! Elijah already knew God would fulfill His promise; the cloud merely confirmed that the rain was on its way. Not only was the rain coming, but it was coming in abundance. What I see, close at hand, is another deluge, a flood. The first confirmed case of COVID was on December 14, 2020, just a little over 3 years ago. If history is to repeat itself, let it be a repeat of the

"Abundance of Rain," during the time of Elijah after three- and one-half years of drought.

Whenever there is an absence of one of the necessities of life, action must be taken. When this same principle is applied to the Church, it is imperative that God use someone to call things into order. Many great men and women were used by God throughout the Bible to teach us these principles, but none greater than Jesus. Jesus had a way of making crooked paths straight. He was always way out in front, putting the Sadducees and Pharisees to shame with His wisdom. He set things in order with just the simplest of words, like when He said, "Martha, Martha." Jesus recognized the principle of first and the importance of one. He knew that Martha was missing what was most needed in her life, which was to sit at His feet. Just like He knew when He spoke to the rich young ruler and told him, "Only one thing is needful, go and sell all that you have and give to the poor."

When asked by His disciples in John 4:31, ***"Rabbi, are you not going to eat?"*** Jesus said, ***"My meat is to do the will of Him who sent Me."*** (John 4:34). He knew His purpose, and like the beam of a laser light, He stayed on course, not deviating to the right or to the left, nor did He run after the latest church fad or the new thing. I do not want to insult the intelligence of some, but there is a subtle seduction happening that few will see. It is subtle because it has the semblance of something spiritual, when in fact it is not spiritual at all. It has a sound, but it is not the sound of Heaven. Most believers are smart enough to recognize a blatant assault from the enemy, but few pick up on the subtle persuasion pulling them from their purpose. If faith is the foundation, then purpose is what propels us! Excuse the alliteration, but purpose is powerless without passion, and it is passion that drives us to pursue something, in this case, the rain.

Subtlety is the devil's strategy! The "Hath God said?" approach has worked well for the enemy. How many have fallen prey to the lying spirit of the devil? How many have believed his lies and followed after his promises of success, fame, and fortune, only to soon find themselves lying on the ash heaps of life? Throughout the pages of this book, I will interject its purpose, so that we stay on track with what I believe the Lord is saying to us, "Let Judah Rise." All that we see can be traced back to a crack in the armor of the Church, an opportunity for the enemy to dull our senses and blind us to the subtle demise and dilution of our once potent lives.

This strategy worked in the Garden of Eden, and it still works today. Have some bought into the damnable doctrines of the devil? Have we exchanged the truth for a lie? What tranquilizing drug has been injected into so many of our churches and preachers that we now place greater emphasis on what some see as ecclesiastical oneness than we do on the Great Commission itself? What is this pursuit of coming together, when in fact it should be a pursuit for God, which makes us one already. The body cannot be fragmented, as the Church is the body of Christ. In Matthew 16:18, Jesus said, ***"I will build my Church and the gates of hell cannot prevail against it."*** Some pastors are acting as if the hand is detached from the arm, but it cannot be so, because we are the body of Christ. Even at Calvary, not a bone of Jesus' body was broken. Anyone who truly walks with God knows that unity is not standing in circles; it is running in a linear pattern that takes us from where we are to where He wants us to be.

Is it possible we have exchanged the great for the good in rounding up our churches with bonfires and sing-a-longs, while forgetting the greater cause. I know I am running the risk of being labeled an extremist, but to be honest, I would be happy to be stereotyped with the many that have gone before me, and those who still run with me, declaring that we have little time left! The cause is greater than the ideologies of those who work to bring churches together but fail to reach the masses. We must have rain!

All of my life I have seen rain fall, but never have I seen anything quite like a tropical storm in Florida. We have all seen rain fall, but few have seen it go sideways. Light rains, with sunlight shining through the droplets, are glorious, but they are certainly far from the spiritual deluge we need in the world today. Our "T-shirt Christianity" is not enough to win this world. It is not what those who fought and even laid down their lives, so that this Gospel could be preached in all the world, wanted to achieve. The "memes" are intriguing, and catch us for a moment, but the reality is our "cruise ship" quotations fall short of a true expression of the reality of our situation. It is not a cruise ship, nor is it a battleship; it is a sinking ship! Our only hope is found in God raising up a people who will run with the Gospel message, rescuing the perishing, and caring for the dying. Judah must rise, and run toward the battle, embracing the Great Commission.

Soon after I graduated from Bible School, I had the opportunity to spend some time with a man by the name of David Wilkerson. I was in New York City, and we met up in a place called "Spanish Harlem." He had arranged for all the streets to be blocked off and was getting ready, that night, to hold a service right in the middle of one of the roughest areas in the city. I was only maybe 22 at the time, but I knew that there was something about him that I wanted in me. He is with Jesus now, but without a doubt, he would be labeled among those who might be regarded as extreme, and even fanatical. He walked into the drought-stricken areas of New York City, parched and dry from the absence of any heavenly downpour; and without thought of his own life, he preached Jesus to gangs. He became a "rainmaker" for those who were spiritually barren.

When the night ended, he took me by the arm, like a father to a son, and walked with me down a couple of streets in the area. It was dark, but he never showed fear. He seemed to possess something that set him apart from others of his era. At this time, New York City had not yet gone through its transformation. Drugs and gangs were everywhere, murder and violence were at an all-time high; yet he walked like he was in charge, like an ambassador who had diplomatic immunity from any and every assault of the enemy. He would point me to the places where he led gang members to Jesus. He showed me where he led addicts in alleys to the saving knowledge of Jesus Christ. What is it that takes a man from a rural church in Pennsylvania to the ghettos of a drug infested city? What compelled him to risk everything in his personal life and in his ministry?

Could it be that he saw the condition of the land, even back then, just as Elijah had during his time? Elijah saw a land filled with idols, and people worshiping false gods, not just on the streets, but in the temple. Is God, the one who never changes, according to Hebrews 13:8, calling us today, as He did Elijah back then, to make these crooked paths straight, to blow the Trumpet in Zion and to sound an alarm? Today, so many of our modern mega churches sit almost empty, because of weak-kneed preachers, who put more trust in secular science than they do in God. Have our once powerful, pulpit- pounding preachers been replaced with facilitators, seeking to navigate a path through the dilemmas facing our society? We need rain! The evidence of drought is very real. You can see it in the natural, but even more intensely, you can sense it in the spiritual. It was Elijah that went to Ahab and asked him for the opportunity to display the power of God. It was he who stood on Mount Carmel and refused to allow his God to be upstaged by the prophets of Baal. When idolatry was filling the land, Elijah knew the urgency and necessity of a divine intervention. If ever Judah was to rise, this would have been the time and place. These people needed something that no idol could ever give them. Although I am thankful for the few that have tapped into the artesian well of living water that is restoring their once parched parishioners, we still have, before us, a world to reach. Give us the thundering voice of a "Jeremiah" once again in our pulpits and on platforms throughout the land. Give us a demonstration, God, of your fire falling from Heaven, consuming every idol and false god. Oh how it must have shaken the ground to see the fire of God come down upon that altar, consuming not only the sacrifice, but also the wood, the stones, the water and everything around it! Those wide-eyed prophets of Baal surely must have stepped back, just like the devil does when he sees the power of God displayed.

The problem with idols, which are whatever is worshiped other than God, is that they change the order of God's divine plan. God said very emphatically, ***"Thou shalt have no other gods before me."*** (Exodus 20:3). The proper order is always for man to pursue God! Everyone is pursuing something that they consider important, which means everyone is pursuing a "god" of some sort. Did you know that long before you ever began pursuing God, He was pursuing you? Psalm 139:7 is an incredible reminder of the undying pursuit of God toward us. ***"Where could we ever go that He is not there? Where could we hide that He could not find us?"*** God found us when we were lost and on our way to an eternity without Christ. Having found us, He wants all of us and is not willing to share.

Many years ago, while pastoring a church in Canada, I had met a precious Italian family who loved the Lord with all their hearts. The wife came to me one day and said, "Pastor, I have served the Lord for many years, and when I came out of the Catholic church as a young married woman, my husband and I made up our minds that we would never look back." She went on to say that since sitting under our ministry, she had a greater desire to pursue more of God, but she felt that there was something standing in the way. After speaking with her for a while, I asked her, "Is there anything in your home that needs to be dealt with?" She could not think of anything at that moment. She replied, "Our home is a Godly home; our Bible is before us on the table; we pray and read the Word together." Then, all of a sudden, her eyes lit up at the realization that, many years ago, when they were just newly married, she had carefully wrapped up all of her old Catholic statues and stored them in the very back of one of her closets. No doubt the Holy Spirit had revealed this to her, because so many years had passed that they had long since been forgotten.

I told her to go home, take the idols and break them, get rid of them, and watch this hindering spirit that had been holding her back be broken off of her life. She immediately did what I told her to do. She was quick to obey, which is a key to breakthrough. The next time we met, she said she literally felt everything she had previously felt break off of her life and a newfound liberty and freedom in Christ come to her like she never experienced before.

God hates idols! The very reason Israel, a type of the Church today, struggled so often was because the people carried this albatross with them everywhere they went. How could an image made of gold possibly do for them what God had already done? Did they not realize that the great deliverance from Egyptian slavery that they had been promised could only be attributed to something so far beyond anything formed and fashioned by the hands of man? It could only be God, Elohim, the supreme God who put on a grand display to Pharaoh and his armies. No man could deny the existence of God after such a rescue! How could they turn so quickly from such a demonstration of divine Power to the cheap tricks of a magician? God literally crushed the rulers of Egypt with undeniable acts. He broke the back of oppression by an open display of His power, yet still, they defaulted to that which they had grown accustomed to. I have often said, they may have come out of the "bondage" of Egypt, but they continued to carry the "baggage" of Egypt.

When Elijah confronted the prophets of Baal, he was not just dealing with a current situation, he was dealing with a spirit that could be traced back hundreds of years. On Mount Sinai, God branded upon the hearts of Moses, and of the people of God, a covenant. ***"If you obey Me and keep My covenant,"*** God said, ***"You will be a kingdom of priests, a holy nation."*** (Exodus 19:5). And in Exodus 19:8, they accepted the covenant of God. This spiritual contract was ironclad and unbreakable; and all they had to do was to love the Lord their God with all of their hearts. Looking back, one cannot help but wonder why Israel would ever venture back into the very bondage that they had been emancipated from, but when you dig deeper, you realize that Israel's problem was not idolatry; it was a heart problem. Aaron said to Moses that the problem with the people was that their heart was set on evil. The idols were just another one of the many "heart issues" that they dealt with.

Come back with me now to Elijah. He had conquered the prophets of Baal, he had seen the miraculous provision of God at the brook Cherith. Ravens had fed him supernaturally and a widow woman had given him her last meal. Now it was time for the drought to end.

It is time for this nation to come out of the drought and see the rain fall one more time upon America. In the midst of all that is taking place in this land, there are glimpses of hope, enough to remind us, again and again, that not only the God of Israel, but also the covenant He had with the Israelites, are for us today as well. Although small in number compared to the population, there are bright lights rising up, who long for the rain to fall. Where are these modern day Elijahs? They can be found with their faces to the ground, calling on the God of Israel to once again display His power. They are the ones who refused to give up, who stood tall when others were running in fear, embracing fabricated scientific reports with a grip tighter than they ever could have grasped God's truth. True Christians do not yield to fear just because their leader is up on the mountain, like the children of Israel did with Moses. He had not abandoned them, and God has never, ever abandoned us. He has been here all along. So why was there a need for a "golden calf?" The golden calf represented just another one of their many acts of rebellion. From the Red Sea all the way to

Mount Sinai, they had complained about the lack of water and the lack of food, and this pattern followed them all through their journey. It was God who spoke to Moses and told him that these "stiff-necked" people were up to something and that he needed to go down from the mountain. Because of Moses's absence from them, the Israelites wanted Aaron to form a golden calf, as a tangible presence of God, when they perceived that God was not around. As if to say that, "If we do not see God or feel His presence, we will make something that will put our hearts at ease." People will worship a god, and if they refuse or reject the only true God, then they will manufacture a god.

With all that has transpired in Christendom, not just over the past few years, but even going back several decades, the pattern of Jewish history seems to continue to repeat itself over and over again. Much like our forefathers, if we do not see God, we tend to try to make something that is symbolic of Him, something to appease us whenever we are frustrated that God did not answer our prayers or show up when we needed Him. It is that subtle deception that has led men and women who once walked close to God, to a place where they have grown satisfied with a semblance, a likeness of God that is no God at all.

Our Sunday morning services, with the exception of the few, are satisfied with a semblance and gladly accept a "likeness" of God in His absence. Many, in fact, have become quite skilled in the art of presenting a Godless gospel, packaged in choreographed sensationalism, with just enough technology to move the masses into a modern day stupor that has a form of godliness but is void of power, with no demonstration, no signs and wonders, and no miracles. We need the rain! We need the rain to fall upon our pulpits and pews, on our city streets and rural communities, and on our courtrooms and our classrooms. We need the rain!

Rain is no respecter of persons; it just falls, and everything within its reach either gets wet or runs for cover. Rain saturates the thirsty, bringing life to the dry, parched, barren soil of our hearts and restores hope in even the very most destitute situations. With his head bowed to the ground, we see now why Elijah so desperately called on God, as he saw the condition of the land. The effects of the absence of rain upon the land for almost three and one half years had taken its toll. Elijah knew that if this went on much longer, the people would not survive, the crops would fail, and the cattle would perish. We need rain!

It was at this critical point in time that Elijah sent his servant to look and see if there was anything upon the horizon yet. Upon his return, the report was not good, as there was no rain in the servant's sight. Maybe we should build a golden calf. I mean, after all, that is the pattern of these nomadic wanderers, known as the children of Israel. "Go again!" was the command, and "keep going. Don't stop until you see something!" Elijah knew that his servant needed to see something, but the prophet of God had already heard a sound, not even an audible physical sound, but a sound by faith, of an abundance of rain. Elijah said to Ahab," I hear it, the sound of an abundance of rain."

Elijah urged Ahab to get up and eat! He reminded him that he did not have to live in a drought-stricken mentality any longer, as rain was on the way. The young servant returned, this time for the seventh time, and said, "I see it." The servant's role was simply to obey and report. Yes, it was small, but it was there, a cloud not much bigger than a man's hand. Though centuries have passed since that memorable moment in time, it still resonates in the hearts of men and women who truly hunger and thirst for the Church to rise to its rightful place of dominion and authority. So small was the cloud that some of the religious crowd would write it off as meaningless and non-eventful, but Elijah knew what was coming. He heard the sound before he saw the cloud, and he activated things before a drop of rain ever fell. Get up and eat! Yes, the famine is about to end; the rain is about to fall; and God's people will once again see the same hand of God that delivered them time and again from the hands of oppressors like Pharaoh, and even from mistakes of their own choosing.

When we understand Godly order, even in a time of chaos, we begin to realize what it means to "Let Judah Rise." There is a sound, heard by faith by all those who believe the promise of God. Let Judah Rise!

CHAPTER FOUR

It Starts Now!

See then that ye walk circumspectly, not as fools, but as wise, redeeming the time, because the days are evil.

Ephesians 5: 15 & 16

Everything inside of me wanted to jump up and shout, but I knew it was not thc right place to do so. I had been asking the Lord for something and, in a setting that would probably have gotten me in trouble, He gave me the answer. I was praying and asking God for a Word in season, an on time Word, that would give me my ministry benchmark for the coming year. The song line from a movie had really impacted me, and I knew, as soon as I heard it, that God, in some crazy strange way, was speaking directly to me, when the Holy Spirit said, "It Starts Now." It was a little difficult at first, because I was expecting God to take me to my Bible, have it fall open to a certain page, and then direct my eyes to the exact chapter and verse; or maybe I would have an epiphany of some sort or some sign; but it did not happen that way. It happened through a song that was not even a Christian song. My initial response was, "Could God speak through something outside of His Word, something I heard in the song line of a movie, a secular movie at that?" And He said, "Of course I can, I am God, I can do anything I want".

I have learned over the years that when the Lord speaks, write it down and take action as quickly as possible to what He says. I am the type of person who must immediately move upon anything the Lord shows me. If something can be done right then and there, you can be sure I will do it without delay. All of my staff knows, that if you even come into a meeting with me without a notepad, pen, iPad, iPhone and if necessary, a whiteboard, you might as well turn around right then and there and return better equipped, because you can be sure there will be some things you will need to write down; so, come in ready. I could not even begin to guess how many projects, directives, assignments, and workflows we go through each week in the ministry, but I estimate it to easily be in the hundreds. Needless to say, our ministry is busy, but my position is always the same, "Do it now." We laugh at some of the things we say amongst our staff, but one of them is "slow walker, slow worker."

Maybe I have a form of undiagnosed attention deficit disorder, or it could be that I just believe so strongly in the importance of redeeming time. The first conference I ever attended in ministry, almost forty years ago, was on time management, and it was probably one of the greatest conferences I ever took part in.

When you consider the average lifespan to be about 79 years, that gives us about 29,000 days. That number gets smaller when it comes to productive workdays; so when you take account of time in this equation, it is a sobering reality, when we think of how much Kingdom work we still have yet to do and of how very little time we have to do it. Younger readers may not quite see it this way, but as we grow older, time is more precious, and often feels more scarce.

Yes, there is a sense of urgency, as eternity races towards us, to gather the harvest with expediency. John 4:35-38 says, ***"Say not ye, There are yet four months, and then cometh harvest? behold, I say unto you, Lift up your eyes, and look on the fields; for they are white already to harvest." And he that reapeth receiveth wages, and gathereth fruit unto life eternal:***

that both he that soweth and he that reapeth may rejoice together. And herein is that saying true, One soweth, and another reapeth. I sent you to reap that whereon ye bestowed no labor: other men labored, and ye are entered into their labors." Years ago, I had the opportunity to travel from where we lived to another city to minister. As I drove to our destination, I looked out into a wheat field. It was a large field, but not more than a few hundred acres. I saw large combines harvesting the wheat, and although I had seen this before, it was the first time I had seen them three or four side by side. It was early in the morning, and my initial thought was how quickly they would get the job done with such massive harvesting machines. On my return trip home later that night, while passing the same field, I saw the lights of those same combines still working, still side by side, and still unfinished! It reminded me of the incredible work we have to do to bring in the harvest for the Kingdom. There is no time to sit idly by and wait, while the harvest is ripe and ready.

Every day of our lives almost 165,000 people die, 6,900 per hour, 115 per minute and about two people per second. Death is unavoidable, and outside of the rapture of the Church, it is the way every person will leave this earth. Hebrews 9:27 says, ***"And as it is appointed unto men once to die, but after this the judgment."*** This puts into perspective the urgency of the hour in which we are living; we must redeem the time!

Most people today live day-by-day, with little regard for eternity. We make so many plans for the very brief period of our retirement years, but few plans for what is to come after we leave this earth. James said that this life is but a vapor that appears for a little while and then quickly vanishes away. Have you ever watched the spark of a bonfire as it breaks forth into the sky, tracing its movement only to see it quickly disappear? Have you ever seen a snowflake fall into a stream never to be seen again? These examples give us a picture of how brief life is in the light of eternity. "It Starts Now" was so much more to me than just a theme for another year of ministry. It was a clarion call to arouse those that sleep to wake themselves up and prepare for battle. The enemy is upon us, and unlike Samson, we do not want to find out too late that we are not ready. Now is the time to redeem the lost and to go after the harvest of souls waiting for a demonstration of God's power and mercy.

Billy Graham preached to over 200 million people in more than 185 countries. His message was timeless, powerful, and still relevant today. He preached a message of love to all races, nationalities, and cultures. The message of the Cross of Calvary transcends all barriers and denominational differences and stands the test of time, pointing millions to Jesus Christ; but if it lies dormant and unspoken, then how shall they hear? The ultimate goal of humanity should be to prepare for eternity, and to see this temporal life as but a brief journey while on the way to our forever home. We only have this day, as tomorrow is not guaranteed to us, so whatever we are called to do, we must do quickly. "It starts now."

When Israel was preparing to engage in battle with the Benjaminites for the wrong they had done, they asked God who should go first, and God's response to them is the same response to us today, "Send Judah first." Nothing in relation to the battles of the past or the battles that now confront us will ever change God's strategy; it will always be to send Judah first. Did you know it is possible to know God's strategies and still lose the battle? That is what happened to Israel. Their first two engagements ended in total defeat and death. It might have been that although they knew that the strategy was to, "Send Judah first," they may not have heeded an even more important part of the plan, which was to always put God first in every facet of life. Praise is one of our most powerful weapons, but if it has become more of a strategy than an experience with God, we are likely to wind up with the same outcome as Israel did against the Benjaminites. A lot of churches and believers today are enamored by the music and the praise and all that goes along with it, but are they enamored with God? To be "enamored" by something means to be in love with it or captivated by it. Is it possible that some have been captivated by praise and worship, not even realizing that they are missing the object of their affection? Have many, today, have become worshipers of worship rather than worshipers of God?

Years ago, at Elim Bible Institute in upstate New York, a prophecy came forth that seems to have greater relevance today than ever before. This is because never, in the history of the Church, have we had more exposure to "Christian" music. So much of it is amazing, truly anointed and inspired by the Holy Spirit; but unfortunately, a significant percentage of these songs are nothing more than just music, with lyrics that talk about God but fail to exalt Him. The prophetic warning was that there would be a greater emphasis on praise and worship than there would be on the Word of God. So allow me to break this down for you. Praise and Worship is such a powerful gift God has given His Church to exalt Him, to lift up His name; and in turn, it is part of the victory we have in two areas, first, in winning battles and second, in bringing in the harvest. In John 12:32 Jesus said ***"If I be lifted up, I will draw all men unto Me."*** What a great promise we have! All that we have to do is simply worship God and watch Him work. But it is not quite that simple. In this, we must be mindful that God has also made it known to us that the Spirit and the Word will never contradict one another; they must be in agreement.

Take for example you and I. We look forward to one day spending eternity in Heaven; and if the truth be told, many long for Heaven to see their loved ones who have gone on before them, but fewer say they long to see Jesus. When questioned, of course we would quickly respond by saying, "Oh yes, I can't wait to see Jesus," but often that is not our first response. That is a snapshot of the problem with Israel; they knew the power that God was speaking of when He said, "Send Judah first" but forgot the object of their worship, God Himself. With God, all things are possible. Praise is simply the catalyst that draws us closer to God, but ultimately, only God can give us the victory. It is not a song, no matter how powerful it is, that defeats the enemy; it is the God of the song. Praise brings us into God's presence, and it is God's presence that destroys the very works of darkness.

This was exactly what Stanley Frodsham was saying way back in 1965. He was warning us that we must not allow our music, our praise, or our worship to become the object of our affection. We must guard against worshiping worship! Rather, the prophetic mandate was to build our lives upon the Word of God, which is God Himself. Why did Israel lose the first two battles, only to find victory in the third attempt? The children of Israel assumed that because God said, "Go up," they were assured victory. When you do not have respect and adoration for God, you begin to assume that things will go in your favor. God said, "Go," but He did not tell them He would deliver the enemy into their hands. When David went to battle against the Philistines, he first asked God, "Shall I go up to the Philistines and will you deliver them into my hand?" God's response to

David was, ***"Go up, for I will doubtless deliver the Philistines into thine hand."*** (2 Samuel 5:19)

David respected and loved God so much that he did not assume anything. It was not until the third battle that the children of Israel prayed, fasted and sacrificed unto God, that He spoke to them and said, ***"Fear them not, for I have delivered them into thine hand."*** (Joshua 10:8). We cannot assume, by praising and worshiping God, that victory is assured. There will be times when we must hear the Lord say to us, "Go up, and I will deliver them into your hands." It is a Word from the Lord that assures us victory.

The rush to conquer the enemy must first be preceded with being in right position with God, situated in a place of prayer, fasting, faithfulness, and obedience, wholeheartedly seeking to hear from the Lord. Not just assuming that if we send praise first, we will win, but actually hearing from the Lord, then moving forward in confidence that the Lord will surely give us the victory, "Let Judah Rise."

CHAPTER FIVE

The Dance Of Freedom

Therefore Michal the daughter of Saul had no child unto the day of her death.

II Samuel 6:23

Just the sound of the word "barren" can be troubling. It brings with it a plethora of thoughts and feelings that seem to make their way to the very core of our being. We are designed to produce; it is part of the creative handiwork of God in our lives, and anything less can be troubling. We often equate barrenness with the inability to give birth, but it goes well beyond that. It is actually defined as "incapable of producing" or "sterile." Living with the stigma of being "fruitless" or unproductive is not only difficult to accept, but it is also not how God designed us to be. God has, from the very beginning in the Garden of Eden, commanded us to, "Be fruitful and multiply," and yet in the story of Michal, she is tragically condemned by David to live a barren, fruitless life from that day until the day she died. What was it in David that caused him to speak such a tragic verdict over Michal's life? "Barren, all your days you shall be," fruitless and incapable of producing anything, from that moment of mockery to the very day she dies. Of all people, David seemed to have an insight into worship that few have known. David had learned something, in his early days, that brought him into a relationship with God, unlike anything seen in other Old Testament characters. Could it have been the countless hours he spent writing songs of worship? Was it that when he felt threatened, his first response was not a reaction to the situation but a recognition of his Heavenly Father?

When David stood in front of Goliath, he knew this to be an impossible engagement unless God was with him. David knew that to win, he could not just depend upon his skill, but he must also have to depend on His God. But like many before and after him, David too had his moments of weakness. His failures are plainly written in Scripture for all to see. This moment in time, when he stood dancing before the Lord, was birthed out of a tragic situation. A man had died for what seemingly looked like a proper response, when the Ark of God crossed the threshing floor. David's heart was troubled, angry, and fearful. A flood of emotions must have been hitting him all at the same time, and he made a mistake. He allowed his emotions to lead him, rather than his love for God, running and leaving the Ark of God at the house of Obed Edom. It did not take long for David, after seeing the blessing of God come upon Obed Edom's house, to realize, "I must return the Ark to its rightful place." Here, David had a fresh encounter with God bringing such joy; in fact, so great was his joy, that he danced with all his might before the presence of the Lord.

Do not be surprised when your joy causes others to despise you. God's blessing has a way of turning some people's hearts against you, inviting jealousy and envy and even, like in this instance with Michal, shame, because they do not understand how you can be so happy. This may be why the Bible tells us to bless them that curse you; probably because God knows they are going to need it. When Michal despised David in her heart, the curse of barrenness was placed upon her life from that moment until her death.

History records periods of time when "barrenness" was in the land, and seasons when absolutely nothing was being produced. Farmers understand barrenness when the lands are incapable of producing crops. We do not always comprehend why we experience barren times and seasons of difficulty, but we do know that, if we apply the principles of God's Word, He can keep us in those times or bring us through those times. Either way, we remain victorious. When we obey God's Word, it protects us from the unseen elements that want to keep us unfruitful. God told Adam to work for six days, but on the seventh day, to rest. What was the purpose of this? It was not just so the soil could replenish itself, but more importantly so man would set aside time to spend with God. God instituted the principle of the "tithe," and said to set apart ten percent of all that you have and return it to the Lord. Why is this principle so vital? It was certainly not because God needs the money, but because God desires to see the obedience and love in the heart of His people to listen to and obey His voice. Not obeying God will always lead to some form of barrenness.

There was a time, in church history, when for almost 400 years, there was no prophetic voice, and nothing new was coming to the Jews from God. Known as the 400 silent years, it must have been unsettling to have once heard from God, and then nothing for such a long period of time. We need to have a prophetic voice to navigate through life. The Bible tells us where there is no prophetic voice, the people perish, live unbridled and are cast off. In the absence of God's presence, chaos and crisis will become the norm. Much of prophecy is a proclamation from God giving direction to us, keeping us from calamity and barrenness. David was responding the right way, while Michal was responding in the wrong manner. The wrong response will cost you!

There is a price to pay, whenever something holy is touched. In Michal's situation, she touched David, the servant of the Lord. The Message translation of this story records David saying that he would gladly look foolish for dancing in the presence of the Lord. What joy must have filled David's heart to know that the thing he was pursuing was now back in its rightful position. God knew that the spirit that was upon Michal was not the Spirit of God working in her, but rather the spirit of her father, Saul. Saul hated David, sought to kill him, envied him, and despised him so much that he threw a javelin across the room trying to end David's life. When we think of the power of our praise, and what it means to send Judah first, it helps us to understand why the enemy will do anything he can to stop us.

There are still some areas in Scripture where the blank spots can be frustrating, but God did not leave us with an incomplete Word. He gave us enough to know Him and His plan for our lives. Michal's story did not stay with her, but rather, it has infiltrated the pages of history and infected the lives of many over time. Yes, just like Michal, we have believers today who are barren, not producing anything in their lives, because they fail to understand what David experienced in his heart, as he danced before the Lord. Some call it extreme, others excessive and unnecessary, but God calls it praise. God never gave us stories in the Bible to point out the faults of the individual or people group. He gave them to us to learn, to reflect, and to guard ourselves from falling victim to the very same thing that incapacitated our predecessors.

As we draw closer to the coming of the Lord, I see God increasing Himself in our lives to the point where, we, too, will be so overcome by His presence that no dance will ever be enough to thank Him for all that He has done. Some are there now, and others are on their way, but too many still struggle to get beyond themselves, and like Michal, look down with disdain, ashamed of the antics of such a person. David's life was much like an open book to the readers of Scripture, but there are still blank spots that we can fill in with our own thoughts of what he might have been like. This in no way dilutes the potency of Scripture; it just lets our imagination go a little beyond what is known and explore what we envision a man like David to be like. What made him so radical, so explosive in his praise, so vibrant when in God's presence?

It may have something to do with what God allowed to happen in his life. Even in the bad things in life, there is something to be learned, and David had a few of those experiences. It was when he had stepped into his role as the second king of Israel, but the first king chosen by God. Anointed by Samuel from the sons of Jesse, David was now in position to bring Israel back to where it should have been spiritually. Israel was a nation of people just like you and I. They were called to follow after God, yet so often their carnality and hedonism became more important to them than God. In a time of vulnerability, the Philistines defeated Israel in war and took the Ark of the Covenant from them. This same strategy of the devil plays out almost every day in the lives of Christians. There is an ongoing battle, and Satan's relentless pursuit of your soul is his ultimate goal. However, unlike the Ark of the Covenant, your soul, once lost in eternity, can never be returned.

Losing the Ark of the Covenant to the enemy was Israel's albatross. They were now without God's presence and power in their camp, and David knew that as the new king, he could not reign with such a void. What it must have felt like to be surrounded with the opulence of the kingdom and all of the luxuries of life! Even while reigning as the king of Israel, a position of such prestige, with servants catering to his every need, David knew in his heart that it was all meaningless if he did not have God's presence in his life. As a child, David knew the anointing, and even in his times of weakness, he remained convinced that God's presence was the most important thing Israel needed the most. Being a Christian requires us to be in continual pursuit of the One who gave us purpose for being. David was God's leader to the nation of Israel; but even today, his legacy continues to serve us, as an example of the rise and fall, the ups and downs, and the victories and failures of man. He is the one that almost each of us can identify with in one way or another, not to justify our shortcomings, but to inspire us to stand back up and run the race.

If Judah is to rise and lead, as God intended, we must be willing to put order into the things that the enemy has sought to destroy. Any man or woman not willing to walk away from everything to follow God is not fit for the Kingdom of God. As harsh as that sounds, it is God's way of articulating His seriousness about first principles. Surely, David modeled this, when he demonstrated that his love for God was greater than his love for his wife Michal. It makes one wonder what people must have thought, when they realized that their king was willing to look foolish, to the point of being mocked and ridiculed, all because of his love for his Lord.

Every one of us is born with or inherits certain gifts, skills or talents, and yes, some are learned over time. One of the talents that seemed to evade my life was in the area of dance. Some people just seem to have the inherent ability to dance, while others do not. I have learned to live with this gift absent from my life. It may be true that lessons could have helped, but other things seemed more important to me than learning how to dance, so I chose the path that omitted the dance instruction.

Having said that, I have felt an unction come upon me many times, as I was overcome with the presence of the Lord. This may not make sense to every one of you, but in praise, there comes a time when tapping your toe is not enough. Clapping your hands is good, but it still falls short of fully expressing what you are truly feeling inside. It has helped me to reflect on how David must have felt, when such joy and excitement came over him that day and brought him to a place where nothing was too much or too good for his God. Was it out of control? It most certainly would have seemed so to the average onlooker; but David was in his element, unaware or just not caring, about who was watching, looking, or for that matter, scoffing at his unbridled love for God on the dance floor that day.

"And David danced before the Lord, with all his might." (2 Samuel 6:14).The picture of that alone could go a thousand different ways, but I see it as a man totally consumed with his God. A man so in control, yet out of control in this one area. Picture him for just a moment, dancing, waving his hands, and shouting, with sweat pouring down his face. His servants had now cleared an area around him creating a circumference of celebration. The people in his Kingdom needed to see this.

David had not been himself for some time, in fact, ever since that man named Uzzah had died. They needed to know that anything they had or were was only because of the God that David worshiped. David had to be the sacrificial dancing lamb, so that he could either be envied or despised. But either way, the Israelites were going to know that God was the center of all things in their nation. The Ark had returned, the king was in his glory, and Israel now was restored to its rightful place in alignment with God's divine order.

Much of the Church today has been consumed in worship, but I am not sure that we have been consumed with God. Think about what the psalmist said in Psalm 67, ***"Let the people praise thee oh God, let all the people praise thee. Then shall the earth yield her increase: and God, even our own God shall bless us."*** With all the Christian music, praise concerts, and church services we have week after week in America, you would think that there would be an even greater deluge of spiritual rain falling upon the dry parched ground of this nation. Is it wrong to expect what the Word of God says? Are we to just hope and wait, or should we not in our hearts know that when we offer to God a praise like David did, then something will happen. Praise activates something spiritually. Lord, bring us to the place where, regardless of where we are, whatever the setting may be and no matter who is watching, let us praise You. Brand our hearts with the revelation of a rain so great that nothing in the natural will impede our spiritual passion for You.

Have great miracles evaded us? Have powerful life-altering revivals passed us by, all because we did not know that just pressing in a little bit more would break the cloud ceiling to the supernatural? Can we not see that it will take a willingness to be despised to demonstrate to God our passion for His presence? Is our fight for freedom not worth it? David knew this, but he did not keep it to himself. David allowed himself to be the sacrificial lamb in a demonstration of freedom that is made available to you today. Dancing, yet despised, was David's story. So many today will forfeit the dance of freedom, fearing it may risk their popularity or the applause of people, when in fact if we allow ourselves to be free like David, the balconies of Heaven may just be filled with onlookers, cheering us on. Have some chosen to hear the chanting of the crowd more than the still small voice of God? Are some so fleshly that they would even be willing to forfeit God's best because of the people around them? Jesus never sought to appease the crowd, He led the crowd, and the people followed Him, not the other way around. Even more, there are "Michals" in our churches today that see our passion as parody and our exuberance as excess. Has denominationalism so dumbed us down to a place in Christianity where what we once called "having church" is now ritualistic and predictable, void of a true demonstration of God's power? Is it possible that we even have some "Michal's" in our pulpits who have turned what we once called a "Holy Desk' into a pub table of round table discussion of doctrinal debates.? Are some of our preachers so empty and void of the oil of the Holy Spirit that platforms have become a place of pomp, props and performance rather than an altar of sacrifice? Was Michal so bad, or was she possibly just like many who fill the seats in our sanctuaries, with an opinion rather than an open heart?

We need to "dance again." Dance in spite of the opinions of others, dance without regard of the onlookers and scoffers. Dance, like the saying says, "like no one is watching" but God. Like the lost coin, the lost sheep and the lost son, we need to rejoice in the recognition that our position in God is never complete until the Ark is back in its rightful place. The coin that was found completed the garment; the sheep that was found completed the flock; and the son who was found completed the family. Israel was empty, just another one of the many nations in Old Testament history, when the Ark was not where it was supposed to be. Some churches are nothing more than architectural monuments, museum-like displays of lifeless statues and storage units for unread Bibles. These types of churches, which are characterized by dogmatic decrees and religious rituals, are attended by their parishioners more out of duty than desire. But when God's presence is ushered in by the praise of His people, these once lifeless brick and mortar buildings become filled with the glory of the Lord; where the cloud of His presence is so strong that flesh dies and carnality ceases to exist. Where God is welcomed and not despised, the "dance" is a normal response, not a rare event that the religious would call extreme. When we invite and welcome God in our services, He shows up, eliciting the visible demonstration of our exuberance about His presence. Hence, dancing is a normal response, and not at all what pious religiosity would dismiss as extreme.

Rise Judah, dance and praise your God with celebration and jubilation, knowing that the Ark is coming down the road! Rise with the expectation that the latter will be greater than the former! Rise with the knowledge that God's promise to his Prophet Joel is nearer than ever before, a day when the rain of heaven will fall, not in little droplets, but like a deluge of glory upon all flesh!

The story of Michal, as sad as it is, should help us to realize that David had insight into a very powerful revelation. While Michal, as Saul's daughter, had her father's spirit upon her life, David had the spirit of God upon his. Consequently, not only was David not willing to risk his legacy, but even more importantly, he was not willing to bring an impure mixture to the holy things of God by fathering children who did not come from a union that glorified God. Each generation that has allowed anything less than God's best has opened the door for the diluted pseudo-gospel message we hear being preached in some of our churches today.

This unholy impure mixture, that is the direct result of compromise in the hearts of God's people, has limited God's ability to operate supernaturally in our lives. It happens because it happened to Jesus, in Nazareth, where no mighty miracles could be performed because of unbelief and impure mixtures of faith and fear. If Jesus could not perform mighty miracles because of the people's unbelief, what makes us think that we would not face the same consequence when we favor fear over faith?

Let Judah Rise to her rightful place in the Church and in the hearts of God's people, restoring all that the enemy has taken in these last days!

CHAPTER SIX

When I Cease to Breathe I Will Be Dead

And the LORD God formed man of the dust of the ground, and breathed into his nostrils the breath of life; and man became a living soul.

Genesis 2:7

Early in our ministry I worked with a wonderful young Pastor, with a beautiful family, who had come from a smaller church in the United States to pastor what is considered a mega church in Toronto, Canada. The task of now shepherding thousands of people in a large congregation, in comparison to a couple of hundred in his previous ministry, was a daunting one, which left him feeling more than a little overwhelmed. His stay there was short-lived, but I recall sitting with him, after he had been ministering for a couple of years and being quite surprised when he turned to me and said, "I haven't been able to take a deep breath in two years." What an eye opener that was for me as a younger preacher! For a moment I thought "I hope no one hears him; it would turn people off from the ministry." I soon came to realize that he was burned out, unhappy and wanting to get out of there. Not too many months later, he took the opportunity to make his way back to where he had come from.

Have you ever had the wind knocked out of your lungs? I know that feeling all too well. Not only from playing sports, like getting tackled in football for example, but also from falling off of my roof not too long ago. Yes, I know that sounds crazy. I could not believe it either. I hit the ground so hard that, for a moment, I was actually unconscious, only to awaken to no breath in my lungs. It was the longest I had ever experienced having to gasp for air , and it felt like my lungs would never function properly again. The fall was so hard that it broke my sternum. As you can probably imagine, the excruciating pain, combined with my inability to breathe, left me feeling like probably the closest I had ever been to death. What a feeling of helplessness, when you are fighting to just get air into your lungs. You cannot scream, because you have no air; you cannot run, because it just immobilizes you; and so you lie there, helpless, until slowly, over time, you come around to being able to catch your breath. I have seen the same glassy-eyed stare of a person who has had the air knocked out of their lungs in the eyes of believers who just feel like they have done all that they could do. They are left wondering, "What is next, God? What does the future hold for me?" Much like in the introductory story of this chapter, my response would be, "Breathe again."

Breathe again that life-giving breath of God into your lungs! What ails you is temporary; fresh wind is coming; new life into your deflated lungs will help to give you a new perspective on all that God has for you. It is not over, and whoever counted you out cannot count! So start now, with shallow breaths in and out, until you are once again breathing at full capacity! The brain can only survive a short time with no oxygen, five, maybe ten minutes at most, before irreversible brain damage occurs. After one minute, brain cells begin to die, after three minutes brain damage is likely and after ten minutes, it is doubtful that the victim will ever recover. The one exception to this is interesting. Dr. Tisherman, and his team at the University of Maryland School of Medicine, found that if the body becomes very cold, it can survive longer without oxygen. Have many people grown cold? How many have allowed the enemy to pull them away from the fire of God, only to find themselves now depleted of the very oxygen they need to keep them alive? Could it be that God is preserving those who have grown cold, keeping them from a more permanent condition, or even from death, because He knows that new breath is coming? How many more minutes will pass before we realize the urgency of breathing again?

Your lungs do not take time to consider the situation going on around them; they do not care; they just want to breathe again. As long as you have breath, you are alive; and as long as you are alive, God has a plan and a purpose for your life. The lyrics of a song we sing at my church says, "If you're not dead, then I'm not done." How true this is for each one of us! There is still much work to do, and so much God wants to do in and through you. You are not dead!

Ever since the beginning, in the Garden of Eden, the devil has been trying to steal what God gave man. The enemy of your soul wants your breath, because your breath is what sustains your life. It is only when you cease to breathe, that you will be pronounced dead, and not a moment sooner!

We have been created by God. Out of the many different belief systems of mankind, what we believe in is Creation. *In the beginning...God.* In fact, Hebrew scholars tell us that the very first verse in the Bible is inverted and actually should read, "God, in the beginning." God, who began all things before there was anything, created mankind for fellowship, for relationship with Him. How incredible it is to rest in the knowledge that God, who was there before anything else, is the Creator, the Builder and the Giver of life!

For man to move from dust to life, breath had to be put in his lungs; thus God breathed. It was the breath of God that went into man first, and the indicated response was for man to "breathe out" God. "Adam became a living being," the Bible says! It is most urgent for us to recognize that life originates with God. He holds the power to give life and to take it away, at His leisure. Fortunately, God is a giving God, not a taking God, so His ultimate plan, even as far back in time as the Garden of Eden, has always been to give.

Man's response was a reaction to what he received from God, the gift of life. He breathed life into us, and in turn, we breathed out. One of the most arduous tasks in life, though an often avoided topic, revolves around having to deal with end-of-life issues. In most cases, this involves much work, including securing power of attorneys, filling out legal forms, and choosing whether to enact in DNR or not. Today, we have the capability to keep people alive medically, even when their lungs cease to function. There are incredible stories of men and women who still had much to do, when death stood in the doorway of their lives. But contrary to what some might think, the Church today is not in a medically-induced coma, nor is it on any breathing apparatus. It is not being kept alive artificially to become an organ donor. It is the Church! The Church today is every bit as vibrant and powerful as the day Jesus said the words that inject hope into even the most despondent of hearts, "I will build my Church." The power of the Church is not diminished, and the anointing is in no way diluted. And the belief some hold that the time of signs, wonders and miracles has disappeared is simply erroneous. The Church is more alive than ever before, regardless of what you might have previously experienced or what you have heard others say.

There is however a very real truth that some, within the ranks of the army of God, have sadly become casualties along the way. It is interesting to note that there has been a dramatic rise in breathing issues here in America. It can be a very frightening thing to lose your breath if you have ever experienced this. COVID, COPD, emphysema, and pulmonary embolisms all take breath away from people, striking unimaginable fear in those who are left gasping for air. When we consider this in spiritual terms, we begin to see the picture of what the enemy is trying to do. He wants God's people on spiritual ventilators, incapacitated, unable to perform their divine function or to fulfill the call of God on their lives. If he could, the devil would love to see preachers water down their messages, thus having a much less potent impact on the desperate masses of people who need to hear the truth! People are yearning for more, not less. They are earnestly seeking genuine, authentic truth, along with a demonstration of what God has promised He would do.

Two things that will bring lethargy in the body are an unhealthy heart and lungs that are not functioning at full capacity. Could it be that both of these issues are affecting people in the

Church, and yet they may not even be aware of it? Has time had such an effect on some, that their spiritual energy levels are being slowly depleted? Have we failed to recognize it? First, it is imperative that we learn to discern whether we are functioning at a diminished spiritual capacity, and second, if we find it to be so, that we immediately take corrective action. The Bible gives us solutions, a remedy to cure weak hearts or lungs. Isaiah 40:31 assures us that, ***"They that wait upon the Lord shall renew their strength."*** God is calling His Church to run these final few meters of the race with a renewed breath in our lungs, so that we can finish this race in victory. Galatians 6:9 serves as a cautionary verse, stating, ***"And let us not be weary in well doing: for in due season we shall reap, if we faint not."***

If God breathed life into us, then life is what flows forth from us. Had mankind initiated the breath, then we could understand why it would be deficient; but because it came from God, we can rest assured that we have everything we need to live a life of influence and spiritual impact upon others.

The battle between the Children of Israel and the Tribe of Benjamin was tragic on so many levels, but most significantly because these were people of the same lineage. Benjamin was one of the Tribes of Israel, and yet the fierce battle in which they engaged resulted in a massive loss of life on both sides. But what started it all? What plots of the enemy, what tricks of the devil were used to turn them against one another? Whenever something unholy touches something holy, something is going to happen. From the Garden of Eden until our present time, God has never tolerated the unholy touching the holy.

In the Garden, the holy thing that was not to be touched was a tree. In the tabernacle, it was a place called the "Holy of Holies." In the Church, it is the Holy Spirit. In your finances, it is the tithe. I think you get the jist of what I am saying. Whenever something unholy tries to touch what is holy, it will always result in conflict. The Levites, who belonged to one of the 12 tribes of Israel known as Levi, held the position of the Levitical Priesthood. They were responsible for transporting the Ark of the Covenant, teaching the law, and performing sacrifices for atonement.

When some from the Tribe of Benjamin raped a concubine from the Tribe of Levi, conflict was inevitable. God made this very clear in James 3:11, when He referenced the inability of both sweet and bitter water to flow from the same fountain. The holy cannot be profaned by the unholy, otherwise the result will always be conflict. The tragedy, in this story, is that the sin of a few resulted in the loss of many, including women and children, innocent lives, all because something holy was touched.

The great spiritual battle occurring today was never meant to be within the ranks of the Church. We certainly understand the battle between sin and righteousness, but we have difficulty understanding why the members of one tribe would fight against one another. The people of God were never meant to be divided by religious differences or denominational boundaries, yet this is entirely too prevalent today. Paul said in Ephesians 4:5-6, that ***"There is one body, and one Spirit, even as ye are called in one hope of your calling; one Lord, one faith, one baptism, one God and Father of all, who is above all, and through all, and in you all."***

Churches should be safe havens and refuges, the hiding place where people; can run to; but so often, conflict arises, even within the walls of our Houses of Worship. Civil wars will always result in the most blood-filled battlefields. The battle was fought, and won 2,000 years ago, when Jesus Christ triumphed over death, hell and the grave, defeating the enemy once and for all. Jesus said in Matthew 28, ***"All power is given unto me."*** At Calvary, the devil was rendered powerless, defeated and dethroned in one swift act from Heaven.

When the Israelites inquired of the Lord, after they found themselves perplexed over the loss of 40,000 men in the war, His response was, "Send Judah first." This strategic maneuver of God not only caused Israel to prevail, but it will also be the very reason you will prevail in every area of your life. Judah breathes out what God has put within us. Judah roars and causes the enemy to tremble. When Judah leads, the victory is always guaranteed, because Judah invites God to the front lines of the battle. The enemy knows that once he sees the Lion of the Tribe of Judah in the front, he has no other option but to flee.

Yes, the Church is the most powerful living institution ever known to mankind. It is, and always will be, the undefeatable militant army that can never be stopped no matter what comes! But is it possible that the Church is unaware of a heart condition or a breathing issue that besets it? Could it be that many have fallen victim to the fainting factor of weariness? Could it be that the ongoing, relentless assault of the enemy, who is forever trying to touch what is holy, has once again subtly deceived entirely too many into yet another lie?

God breathed His very life into Adam, and through Adam into you! That breath must not allow itself to grow shallow, choking your spiritual strength down to a whisper of a tone, when God has breathed into you a shout of victory. You are no longer in need of a breathing apparatus, as new breath has come into your lungs! ***"Let Judah Rise."***

CHAPTER SEVEN

I Never Knew He Left?

And she said, The Philistines be upon thee, Samson. And he awoke out of his sleep, and said, I will go out as at other times before, and shake myself. And he wist not that the LORD was departed from him.

Judges 16:20

Delilah was the bait, used by the Philistines, to finally apprehend their adversary Samson. He had tormented them long enough. They had come to realize that the only way to trap him would be to uncover the secret to his strength. Despite her many tries, Samson always seemed to be able to evade Delilah's devious plans. But her relentless pursuit eventually wore Samson down, and despite his tenacity, his story sadly ended in surrender. Each of Delilah's attempts was futile, as Samson would awaken to easily overcome anything she had tried to do to find the secret of his strength…until one fateful day. Sin is not always an instant fall from living a righteous life to a lifestyle of iniquity. It is often subtle and secretive, slowly working to erode every foundational pillar of truth in your walk with God. Sin disguises itself as something appealing to the appetite of the flesh. Sadly, sin, just like in Samson's story, will cause you to wake up one day and not even know that what you once had is now gone.

That is tragically the case in many lives, those who were once filled with power and anointing, those who once knew God so intimately but now rarely spend time with Him, until they wake one day to find that all that they once had is now gone. How many have been worn down, but not by blatant attacks, but rather by subtle temptations. What we were once convicted by, we are now casual with, drawing us into the slow but sure demise of our lives. For some, it might be the beauty of a woman. Others are enticed by lust for money, fame, or fortune, while yet others are simply the victim of the continual barrage of the enemy upon their lives. No matter how it happens, the end result is always the same. It will leave you in a weakened, and therefore vulnerable, condition, unable to fulfill the call of God upon your life.

'Subtle' is an interesting word, because it can apply to many different scenarios., In some contexts, subtlety can be a positive character trait, while in others it indicates a level of deceitfulness that embodies adjectives like, "crafty, "wily," or "cunning." I could not help but be reminded of a cartoon from my childhood, called, "The Road Runner." If you are familiar with it, you will of course remember his adversary, the coyote. His real name was "Wile E. Coyote " and yes, he was wily, but not so subtle. I like to think of the devil as a kind of "not-so-subtle" foe, who really does not have a chance to take us out, unless we allow him to do so. He knows that we have access to the wisdom of God and once we utilize that, he really has no power over us. If he can wear us down or trick us, like Delilah did Samson, then we may also find ourselves waking up one day to the reality of a powerless, pitiful condition that has come upon us over time.

What could possibly be worse than losing something so valuable that was given to you as a gift? It would be understandable if it had little or no value, or if it was not a necessary or treasured item; but something like Samson had been given was so rare and so special, that to lose it must have been debilitatingly devastating. When you lose something of no value, it is easy to put it out of your mind and move on. But what about something so priceless, that to lose it would be a life-altering blow to you, and even more so, if it is something that you are sure, that once lost could never be replaced, except by the original owner itself? This was the story of Samson. No one had ever possessed the strength he had, which was not only a gift given to him by God but also a solemn vow between him and God. His strength was so great that it had enabled him to tear apart a lion, to carry the city gates away on his shoulders, and to tear the ropes of the Philistines off of his arms like thin threads of string. His name was known far and wide, as he was recognized as the strongest man ever known. As Samson's enemies rejoiced in his weakened state, I cannot even imagine the sorrow those who loved him must have felt to now see him weak. It brought such sadness to those who loved him, but joy to his enemies.

Satan loves watching everything that God loves succumb to his subtle lies. Yes, he takes joy in your demise and revels in hideous laughter, when a once mighty man or woman of faith now finds themselves huddled in the corner of the ring, cowering from the adversary.

"Judah Rise" is about the incredible power we have in God when we send Judah first and recognize the significance of the Lion of the Tribe of Judah; but while we see Jesus as that incredible figurehead, there are times when the devil is referred to as a lion, albeit a defeated one. Having said that, lions have a reputation of being profoundly lazy, and while they do sleep for a good part of the day, they are not lazy. The truth is that they are incredibly patient, not slothful. Because lions are "ambush predators," they lie in wait, knowing that time will bring them what they desire. Generally, lions can usually go three or four days between meals, so they have learned to wait for their prey to come to them. It is also worth noting that lions do not often hide or wait in hilly country or rocky places, but rather, they stay where they know other animals will come, usually a watering hole. It is interesting to see that many of those we find in spiritual decline are those that once thrived at the watering holes we call churches. These once "on fire" believers allowed something to affect them so significantly that it ultimately pulled them away from God, not knowing that the enemy was crouching just outside the doors, like a lion by a watering hole.

Imagine having some kind of a meter or gauge that we could look at daily to monitor our spiritual condition, allowing us to know if we are stronger or weaker each day? But that is not the case. God created man to make his own decisions and choices, allowing us to live with free will. We have been given this attribute, because God loves us so much that He refuses to force us to love Him. Love is never controlled; it is free to make its own choices. No greater love could ever be shown to man, than for His very creator to release him to his own desires. We do not have to serve God, we choose to serve Him, which is the greatest evidence and demonstration of love.

So how could such a powerful man like Samson fall into such a trap? He did not fall out of love with God, but he did fall in love with things that would interfere with his walk with God. One of the areas that I believe we are going to see a rise in these days is a call back to a separated lifestyle. The Bible asks the question, "***What fellowship hath light with darkness.***" (II Corinthians 6:14). It is the little foxes that spoil the vines, and when we allow anything to come between us and God, we can be sure that it signals the beginning of a spiritual death spiral that, without a swift turnaround, will plummet us right into the abyss of hell. God did not tell us to just avoid evil. He told us to avoid the "very appearance" of evil. Yet so many today live their lives to see how close they can get to the edge and still live, while God's plan for us is to see us live far from anything that would bind us with ropes that cannot be broken. Samson woke up, but not like he did on other days. This time he woke up to find that what he once had was gone. Just like then, the enemy is upon us, and many are waking to find that they lack what they need to win.

How do we move from such a depleted spiritual condition to a place of restoration? What does it take to "rise again?" Just because the enemy wins a battle does not mean he has won the war; in fact, he already lost that war at Calvary. To rise again is as simple as making a decision. It is waking up to find yourself weak, but choosing not to stay that way. It is filtering your friends list. It may require the "delete" button to be so active on your social media accounts that sparks are flying off the keyboard. It may even require a change of phone number. Regardless of what it may be, it begins with a decision. If your desire is to truly see God restore all that the enemy has taken from you, a decision is what begins the process.

When Israel was losing and their men were being slaughtered, they made a decision. Their decision was not to get more men or better armor or to devise a more strategic plan. Their decision was to "inquire of the Lord." When everything is failing in you and around you, do what David did: Run to the Rock that is higher than us, run to Jesus. When the Israelites were not only losing, but losing badly, all God said was "Send Judah first." You will see elsewhere in this book that it was not just a matter of sending Judah first, because if we send praise and do not have a relationship with the King it will avail us nothing. It was not until the third battle that Israel prevailed, because this time, the people fasted, prayed and sought God.

The Message translation of the Bible gives a different picture of the story of Samson's life. It tells us that when Samson yielded to Delilah, he woke up not realizing that God had abandoned him. What a shock that must have been! But his life was not over yet. The Bible tells us that the Philistines grabbed Samson, gouged his eyes out, shackled him and put him to work grinding in the prison. So many who have fallen away from God have found themselves here, shackled, blinded and in a place of total abandonment. But God always keeps His covenant.

It was not long before Samson's hair began to grow again. His vow as a Nazarite was to let no razor touch his head, because the secret of his strength was in his hair. The crowd cried out, "Get Samson!" Little did they know what they were about to see. With over 3,000 Philistines gathered in the temple that day, Samson asked his guide to place his hands on the pillars of the temple, the ones that held up the roof. He cried out, ***"God, look on me again."*** (Judges 16:28). Oh, that this would be the cry of those who have fallen away, who have slumped into mediocrity, who have yielded to temptation! God look on us again!

Does God abandon us? Does He leave us? How could He? He promised He would never leave us or forsake us, but He does leave us to fend for ourselves, if we are not walking in obedience. He will leave us to our own desires and our own choices. If we choose Him, then we, like Samson, will leave this world making the greatest impact of our lives. Samson placed his right hand on one pillar and his left on the other and said, “Lord, strengthen me, ONE MORE TIME.” Let Judah Rise!

CHAPTER EIGHT

Reason Or Passion?

And it came to pass, when Moses held up his hand, that Israel prevailed: and when he let down his hand, Amalek prevailed.

Exodus 17:11

Because we live on earth, within the laws of nature, there are laws that govern how we live, put in place by God, such as the law of gravity, for example. We also have laws written by man that fall within the framework of many of God's laws, like the law of thermodynamics, the law of relativity, and so forth. Laws, which govern our land outside of the external force of God, are how we live each day. We also have-man made laws, which are intended to keep civility in our society.

One such law is the law of inertia. Called Newton's first law, the law of inertia states that an object will remain at rest or in uniform motion in a straight line, unless compelled to change its state or direction by an external force. Inertia is, in fact, an object's tendency to resist change. If no force acts against the object, then the object will maintain an intriguingly constant velocity. Many believers today can fit into this category, such as those who resist change who, though they may be admired for their consistency, fall short when it comes to living an accelerated lifestyle. I would suggest that religion is a great trap for this mediocre kind of life, almost comparable to what John said in Revelations 3:15, ***"I know thy works, that thou art neither cold nor hot: I would thou wert cold or hot."*** That consistent pattern is lacking growth because of the resistance to any external force being applied. Many consistent patterns are admirable, like faithful Church attendance, faithful giving, and a consistent prayer life; and while all these are good, to remain in a constant state, unchanged is not how the Kingdom works.

Martin Luther King once referenced what he called "the tranquilizing drug of gradualism," in his historic, "I Have A Dream" speech. I will never forget hearing those words for the very first time. While not necessarily falling under the definition of "inertia," it does also give us a picture of a declining lifestyle, one that has, over time, allowed itself to be affected by either the internal lack of desire to pursue or an external force applied causing a resistance to pursue. Gradually, people slip away. We have all seen them, or even possibly been them, where what was once such a burning passion for God has been replaced by the dimly glowing embers of a once great man or woman of faith.

What is the force that causes such a falling away? As I was walking around one of the buildings on our campus recently, I looked down to see where water had been dripping along one of the outside walls from the rain gutters above. It was a taller room, so the water was falling fifteen to twenty feet down onto solid concrete. When the water came into contact with the concrete, I saw a one-inch hole in the concrete that had been created by the continual drip. It was the gradual, consistent drip of water that, over time, had worn away a portion of solid concrete. How powerful it was to realize that it was not the water that caused the erosion, but rather it was the consistency of the drip!

Our "concrete" Christian lifestyles, as powerful as they may be, are always vulnerable to the relentless and consistent attacks of the enemy. It is inevitable that any true believer will face this in their walk with God. The subtle attacks of the enemy are corrosive in nature. They will eat away at even the most powerful structures, if permitted. The secret to resisting them is a counterattack. The force of sin and the temptation of the devil must be resisted and confronted with a lifestyle defined as "dynamic." I realize this is not a physics book, yet so much of physics can act as a parallel to the Christian life. A dynamic Christian is one who is in a constant state of change, moving in the right direction, which is called "velocity." Velocity is defined as the speed of something, going in a certain direction in a linear pattern. Paul the Apostle said, **"I press toward the mark, for the prize of the high calling of God in Christ Jesus."** (Philippians 3:14). There will always be some form of resistance trying to ultimately stop you from reaching your goal, but Paul's determination overpowered any resistance and took him to the finish line. This is evidenced in II Timothy 4:7, when Paul asserts, ***"I have fought a good fight, I have finished my course, I have kept the faith."***

Few things are more detrimental to the advancement of the Church than when we find ourselves with our arms down at our side and the enemy prevailing over us. Have we gradually allowed our faith to fail, our praise to become passive, and our prayer life to fade into obscurity? Do you wonder why you watch blessing after blessing upon those around you, but fail to have a moment of rejoicing for what God is doing in your life?

If God were to say that one of His laws is simply that if you raise your hands, you will prevail over the enemy, I am sure most would gladly walk around with their hands in the air all the time. This was the story in Exodus 17. Moses became a symbol, a focal point for Joshua to look up to for faith and encouragement. When Joshua looked up to the hill where Moses sat upon a rock, and saw his hands raised, he was not only inspired and encouraged, but he also became convinced that God would give them the victory. Let me again preface the importance of knowing that the Church is more powerful than ever; but have some let their hands down? How simple would it be if it were just a law, if you knew that if you just raised your hands, you would win? As much as God loves to see the passion of His people and honors and rewards our fervency, it is not the only thing that moves the heart of God.

He is empathetic towards his children, but He is a God who functions through His laws.

In Isaiah 1:18, when God called His people to **"reason together,"** He was not drawing them into a debate regarding salvation. He was revealing one of his laws: Though your sins be as scarlet, they shall be white as snow. God is speaking to Judah here and telling them that only He has the right to bring resolution to their problem. He establishes a principle that, if applied, will bring cleansing and sanctification to their sin stained lives.

When Esau sold his birthright because of his hunger, the Bible tells us that he sought a place of repentance with tears and did not find it. Passion is powerful, but it does not change the laws of God

Raise your hands both physically and figuratively! Moses physically lifted his hands; otherwise, he would not have grown tired and needed an Aaron and a Hur on either side to lift his hands for him. Moses knew that if he obeyed God and kept his hands in the air, the Amalekites would be defeated.

Could it really be that easy, that a simple act of obedience could bring victory over the enemy?

I wonder if God looks upon some of our churches today, only to find people with their hands down by their sides. Is it possible that lands you did not own that were supposed to be yours and houses you did not build that God destined for you evaded you because you were caught with your hands down instead of lifted high in the air? Could it be that revival, miracles, signs and wonders that are promised by God for His people are standing off at a distance, waiting for an opportunity to look up to see a "Moses" sitting on a rock with his hands in the air? Is revival really just a matter of making a decision to keep our hands up in the air, so to speak, spiritually?

The Church is powerful, but does it need a, "Let Judah Rise" experience one more time? Has COVID and cancer, calamity and catastrophe so disengaged us from the supernatural that we have difficulty even believing any longer that God can save, heal, and restore?

Everybody wants to win, but few are willing to pay the price of victory. Has inertia gripped our hearts and filled the Church with such fear that it has limited its potential? Has the spiritual sin of atrophy, the gradual decline in effectiveness or vigor due to underuse or neglect, gripped our lives? If so, "Let Judah Rise."

A passionless Church is a powerless Church without a doubt, as we are creatures of passion. It is through the passionate preaching of Christ and Him crucified that men's lives are transformed; yet passion in itself is not enough. There must be an understanding and acceptance of the laws of God. If you praise Him, he WILL inhabit your praise! That is a law. If you give, it shall be given unto you! That is also a law.

In a courtroom, lawyers argue the rule of the law, Judges make decisions based upon the rule of the law, but more often than not, juries are swayed by passion. The passionate plea of a mother or father can sway the heart of a jury, much like prayer can move the heart of God; yet both have their place in the Kingdom.

There is room in this world, in the Christian world, for both law and passion. Aristotle defined law as reason free of passion, yet both have their place in the church. The law works in that regardless of how many passionate tears are shed, or the lack thereof, the law of sowing and reaping will work. Will passionate tears negate the law of sowing and reaping? Not ever, it can only enhance it.

In Psalm 6:6 David said, ***"I water my bed with my tears,"*** yet because of the sovereignty of God, it may or may not make a difference. God has placed things in order, while the devil seeks to bring disorder or chaos into everything God has placed into order. The order of God to Moses was simply, "Raise Your Hands." The flesh grows weary, the spirit can even grow weak, but it is for this reason that God gives us people around us to encourage us in our faith and to lift up our hands when we are weak so together, we can reap the victory.

The opposite of "inertia" is "momentum". Inertia will keep you locked in a continual downward spiral, whereas momentum will release you to the unlimited supernatural miracles of God. When Adam was created by God, there was no "Plan B" in place. God did not create Adam with failure in mind, no more than He created you with failure in mind. He created you to win, to succeed, and to overcome every obstacle in your life. God created Adam with these words in mind, "Be fruitful and multiply." This same promise is what God spoke to Abraham, when He told him that his seed shall be as the stars of the heavens and as the sands of the sea. Yet, just 10 generations into creation, man's heart was desperately wicked. What happened? Spiritual inertia, atrophy? Man grew increasingly wicked, so much so that God repented that He even made mankind upon the earth.

God's plan for His people was generational blessing, that their children and children's children would walk in the increasing blessing of the Lord. Had sin not interrupted God's plan, can you imagine what would have come upon the generations that would follow? Blessing is a law of the Lord. It is God's will to bless His people, but when the flow and continuity of that is broken, God has to find another way, another man who will walk in holiness and integrity to pick up where the last one failed.

We are now many thousands of years past that time in Bible history, and God is still seeking out those who will help carry out His original plan. The plan will never cease to move forward, God will see to that; but He seeks someone who will rise up from the ashes of obscurity and seize this incredible moment in time to let "Judah Rise," possibly just one more time, before the coming of the Lord.

Paul warned us not to grow weary in well-doing! WE SHALL REAP, but we must not faint or be in the process of fainting. Lift your hands again, lift them high, stretch them into the heavens and experience the surge of God's power to defeat every enemy that comes against you. ***"Let Judah Rise."***

CHAPTER NINE

There Is No Middle

I know thy works, that thou art neither cold nor hot: I would thou wert cold or hot.

Revelation 3:15

There is not a military strategist or a general of any great army, nor could there be any truly called preacher of the Gospel who could ever lead their people with half-hearted intentions. These callings and occupations require full dedication, and nothing less will do. When you take on these positions, you must be willing to lay down everything for the sake of the calling. Nothing in God that is not worth dying for is worth living for, so living for God must be with intentionality, determination and perseverance. Lives lie in the balance, humanity is at stake, freedom is compromised, and victory will be evaded, if the heart of a leader is not fully engaged in the purpose for which he is there.

The easiest place to live is in the middle, that comfortable abode between the leader at the top and the ones who serve underneath. Middle is easy! You have a degree of authority, although limited, but do not have to take on any responsibility. Tucked in behind the leader is probably one of the safest, most comfortable environments in which a person can be. There is nothing wrong with being there, unless, of course, you are talking about your spiritual condition. Middle can be children before they reach the age of maturity, who are still getting direction, protection and provision from their parents. They enjoy the safety of that covering, until such time as they are ready to step out into the world on their own. Middle can be an employee who simply takes directions from the boss, or any situation in which one is not the bullseye of the adversary's arrows. In the many conversations I have had with other ministers, I have found that many, who once held positions of leadership, are now quite comfortable with being the "middle man." The pressure is not as intense, the demands on their lives subsides, and all around it is just easier; but easy is not always God's way.

Where the danger lies in leadership is when we make wrong decisions. One decision can bring upon us blessing or curse, which not only affect us, but our seed, or our soldiers. We see, in the life of David, a time when a wrong decision was made. This great king, who once as a shepherd boy had defeated a lion, a bear, and the giant named Goliath, now stood in the place of judgment himself. According to the Bible, David was known as a worshiper and as a man after God's own heart. Through his life story, we learn that one wrong decision does not mean you have walked away from the Lord, nor is it the end of the road in your walk with God. David continued to love and worship God, even after a bad decision, but it was his bad decision that caused him to distance himself from God.

The only way that you can keep your anointing strong and your faith growing is to remain in a continual state of progression with the Lord. A progressive Christian is one who is in a state of forward movement, development and growth. Moving away from God, or as David did, hiding from the Lord, had broken the continuity he once had, thus impeding his progress. David hid in a cave, and Adam hid behind a bush; but no matter where we go, God is there to hold us accountable for our actions, but in His mercy, always with a plan of restoration. The Bible says God did not come to condemn that world, but that the world through Him, might be saved.

When the enemy comes in, and he will, he never comes without an agenda. His plan is always to press you until he breaks your fellowship with God and weakens your spiritual defense system. David made a serious mistake, because he failed to stay close to God. II Samuel 11 tells us that, at a time when kings would go to battle in the Spring, David, instead of joining them, opted to send Joab and his servants. By staying in Jerusalem, David was now in a weakened position and vulnerable to the temptation of the enemy. And sure enough, in just moments, the enemy used this as his opportunity to bring down the king.

It is for this reason that being in that middle place is so dangerous to your spiritual growth and anointing; it is where David was, when he should have been at war. If the past several years have exposed anything in the Church, it has revealed God's true leaders whose faith in God never wavered and exposed those who would bow to the delusions of the world. When everything we are in God should have stood the test, many failed and moved to the middle ground of comfortable acceptance, a place that had a semblance of God but was most certainly tainted with the flesh. Fear replaced faith and men's knees buckled, when they should have stood strong.

The Judah I speak about in this book is a Judah that does not walk in fear but in faith. Several years ago, I was traveling to preach a meeting in southern Africa. I was in a number of countries, including Zambia, Mozambique and Zimbabwe. As I was escorted from church to church, I remember my driver repeatedly pointing out which church was an AFM Church, so much so that the term became very familiar to me. I quickly learned that AFM was the acronym for the Apostolic Faith Mission that was founded by none other than John G. Lake and Thomas Hezmalhalch.

It was Lake who in 1910, in the middle of one of the worst worldwide pandemics, known as the Bubonic Plague, boldly declared his faith. The death rate was so high that they could not recruit enough people, no matter how much the government would pay them, to remove the dead bodies fast enough. In one of the most highly contagious regions during the plague, John G. Lake offered his help, but refused monetary compensation. Lake carried diseased, dying and dead bodies out of houses, often to bury them in mass graves; but through it all, he had absolutely no fear of catching the disease.

Why must we "Let Judah Rise" within us, and within the Church today? This past pandemic of Covid was a test, which many did not pass. If the Church does not rise up, fewer still will pass the tests that are coming in the days ahead, without a genuine encounter with God.

A medical doctor asked Lake, "What do you do to protect yourself?" All Lake said was, "I believe that, as long as I keep my soul in contact with the living God so that His Spirit is flowing into my soul and body, that no germ will ever attach itself to me, for the Spirit of God will kill it." When faith should have annihilated fear, many chose the path of least resistance. Where are those who will stand in the bow of the boat, fearless, not feeling the temptation to run and wake the Master and accuse him of not caring? Where are those who actually believe that their voice has the same power as His voice and are themselves willing to cry out "Peace be still?"

Imagine if many of our spiritual leaders would have taken this approach, what a difference it would have made! Imagine if preachers, rather than shutting down services and gullibly believing the misinformation of unscientific research which elicited a fear-based response, would have just believed what the Bible says and had enough faith to not shut the doors of their churches! I am not judging, but I assure you, that another time of testing will come, another opportunity to show God's strength and power to this world. We pray we do not, once again, fail the test. This was not the only storm the disciples faced, and this will not be the last pandemic we face; there will come another test that will push the limits of our faith in God.

Lake turned to the doctor and said, "Take the foam from the lungs of a dead plague victim and put it on my hand." When the doctor obliged Lake, and then looked at his hand under a microscope, he watched as masses of living germs died instantly. Lake told him, "That is the law of the Spirit of Life in Christ Jesus… When a man's spirit and body are filled with the presence of God, it oozes out of the flesh and the pores, and it kills the germs."

If you have ever asked God for the key to breakthrough or the path to victory, this is it! When you are more filled with God, then you are with fear, it will ooze out of your pores, killing everything in its path that is in opposition to God. Sickness, disease, plagues, pandemics or anything else must yield to that level of faith! Jesus awoke to the sound of the disciples' fear, as they cried out to Him. **"Master, don't you care?"** (Mark 4:38)

Judah rising within God's people, within His Church, is not just something to be considered; it is something we cannot go forward without. We have found ourselves here, in a similar situation, in recent years. "Middle" has hurt us. It has set us back, much like Adam and Eve set back the plan of God until Noah came along. Bible history is filled with setbacks, but nothing can ever stop the advancement of this mighty army known as the Church.

Even though there has been much teaching on the whole topic of spirit, soul and body, misinformation still abounds. When we are in the middle, we are often operating in the soulish realm, rather than in the spirit realm. The soul relies upon our intellect, our emotion and our will, and these areas will tap into our senses, which do not have the capacity to experience God, because God is a Spirit. Our soul wants to recognize God by our senses, to see Him, to feel Him, to hear Him, but the reality is God is not able to be recognized by our senses. God is revealed to us, not recognized by us. It is often in that middle place spiritually that we know *about* God, but do not really *know* Him. We really only fully come to know God, when we know Him in spirit. How I see God can be limited by my senses, but it is unlimited in my spirit. The place called "the middle" struggles in faith to really comprehend how great and how big God really is. Our faith will fail when we limit God with our senses, but when we have a concept of God through our spirit, it is then that our faith becomes limitless. John G. Lake knew this and applied this to his life during a time of testing, and it worked. Faith always works, when it is applied God's way!

Imagine knowing God outside of the limitations of our senses. Judah moves in this realm, where praise penetrates the natural barriers and takes you into unlimited supernatural places. Your finite faith will transform into an inexhaustible faith. Where you were limited before, you will never be limited again, because although the action of lifting your hand in praise is a physical one, it is your spirit that is in direct contact with God's Holy Spirit, divinely connected and in the realm in which nothing is impossible. It is a faith lifestyle, or a faith journey, that is filled with so much of God that no flesh could dare enter in.

Charles Spurgeon once said, "Nobody can do as much damage to the church as the man who is within its walls, but not within its life." Could it be that many who sit in the pews or chairs of our churches have fallen victim to the lifeless experience of living detached from the vine? Once there, they become susceptible to the faithless, unscriptural teaching that permeates our pulpits. This is not where God wants His Church. The Church was never called to be an ecclesiastical enigma, but rather a place where the weary and the wandering can come home, the hurting and the hopeless can be healed, and those bearing the burden of sin, can stop at Calvary to be relieved of all that this world has laid upon them. Not only will Jesus Himself pick up our heavy loads, but He will carry them as far away from us as the East is from the West!

When we find ourselves here, "*in the middle*," we must recognize that we are out of divine order and must find our way home. In Revelation 3:15-16, Jesus said, ***"I know thy works, that thou art neither cold nor hot; I would thou wert cold or hot. So then, because thou art lukewarm, and neither cold nor hot, I will spue thee out of my mouth."*** Jesus was essentially saying that being cold was better than being in the mediocre middle known as lukewarm, which is the most dangerous place for a believer to be. God is calling us to the "hot," the place where miracles happen! Run to the fire, run to Jesus and let the Breath of God breathe new life into your spirit today, ***"Let Judah Rise."***

CHAPTER TEN

May God Be Praised

And she conceived again, and bare a son: and she said, Now will I praise the LORD: therefore she called his name Judah.

Genesis 29:35

Judah, the fourth son born to Jacob and Leah, was head of one of the twelve tribes of Israel. His name means "praise." In Proverbs 22:1, the Bible tells us that, ***"A good name is rather to be chosen than riches."*** There is something powerful to be said in the choosing of a name. Each of our children were prayed over long before they were born, but like most families, we wrestled with the choice of their names. Our daughter Victoria was born in 1994, and like for the others, we had a name chosen for her some time before she was born. I remember it so well; they wheeled my wife into the delivery room, where we waited for the doctor to arrive, and it seemed like in no time at all, we had a new beautiful baby daughter. What was most interesting, though, is that the moment she was born, the Lord spoke to us and said, "Do not call her the name you have chosen, for I have a new name for her." We had already put the name we had chosen on some of the documents and had already made all the plans, but God had another idea.

Today, that young baby girl is now a full-grown married woman, with a strong anointing to preach the Gospel. She knows how to fight the enemy, as she walks in faith, and all these years later, we now see why God had a different name in mind, Victoria, meaning "victory" or "victorious."

When Leah conceived, she named her son Judah and said, ***"Now I will praise the Lord"*** (Genesis 29:35). Often, we predetermine the outcome of events in life based upon natural, visible circumstances. And although there is great power in our words, God often takes us by surprise and uses the most unlikely things for His glory. Out of rejection and pain, Leah gave birth to the very one who would lead people into great victory. Little did she know that from her would come a child, who would become a tribe, who would represent a standard for the Church to adhere to, if ever it was to overcome the enemy. Judah! Oh, what victory is in that name!

The tribe of Judah became the most powerful and the most important tribe in history. From Judah, not only came King David and King Solomon, but Jesus Himself, the Messiah, would come from the lineage of Judah. God invoked great blessing upon Judah and the Tribe that would come forth.

"Judah, your brothers will praise you; your hand will be on the neck of your enemies; your father's sons will bow down to you. You are a lion's cub, O Judah; you return from the prey, my son. Like a lion he crouches and lies down, like a lioness - who dares to rouse him? The scepter will not depart from Judah, nor the ruler's staff from between his feet, until he comes to whom it belongs and the obedience of the nations is his" (Genesis 49:8-10). From Leah's womb, she declared Judah to be set apart. Little did she know that for generations to come, the name Judah would be the very thing that would take the Church into its greatest position of victory. Judah shows up everywhere, hopefully in church services across our nation and around the world; but so much more than that, Judah must be recognized in every aspect of our lives. The psalmist David said, ***"I will bless the Lord at all times, His praise shall continually be in my mouth"*** (Psalm 34:1). When praise is central inside of us, it disarms the devil and aggravates the adversary, as he absolutely despises praise.

"Now I will praise the Lord!" We can read many things into Scripture and are warned to be careful to rightly divide the Word of God; however, could it be that this was the wake-up call to Leah, and the wake-up call to God's people? Are we finally at the breaking point, where the same old, same old will no longer suffice, because it is not getting us the desired results that we so desperately need? Is there another level we have yet to attain, a place we have not been before, where we cannot be denied? What was Leah saying here? Was she saying she had been deficient in her praise, but now she would start? Was she repenting for the lack thereof, or for remorse over her shallow relationship with God at the time? Why now, and why so long before she would finally say, "Now I will praise the Lord?"

Very little of our Christian music today is birthed in the anointing and saturated with God's glory in the incubator of the Holy Ghost. I appreciate the effort and energy that is exerted by songwriters and musicians who truly take time to produce music, but never has there been more music in our world than there is today. So, there is not a problem with a lack of music, but there is, however, a dearth of anointed Heaven opening, hell shaking music that is not only sung by congregations across America but is known by every demon in hell as songs that initiate a move of God.

If a Grammy is our ultimate goal, we have fallen short of God's plan. If a Dove Award or platform recognition is the true desire of our hearts, our motives have missed the mark. These things are deservingly the secondary rewards of hard work, but what the world considers good, God may not. Our pursuit of praise must be void of the desire for earthly accolades and recognition from the music industry and genuinely desire to create an atmosphere, where God invades our space, overtakes our Praise and Worship services, and wrecks our plans, so that He can display Himself to us.

Music is more than notes on a chord chart, sounds from an instrument or vocals through a microphone. Music is a sound from Heaven that invades enemy-held territory, penetrates the darkest of prisons and brings deliverance to captives. Music transcends time and space, breaks through atmospheres, and if allowed, shatters the shackles of the oppressed and tormented.

It was the praise of Paul and Silas that shook a prison cell, bringing freedom to not just some, but all who were bound. What was it that caused the pins of the cell doors to unloose themselves, locks to unlock, blocks to be pulverized into powder? What was it about their praise, that midnight moment, that loosed the bonds that held them? Could it be that the depth of their depravity met the sovereignty of their Savior, accessed by the anointing upon their praise, that dreary day in that Philippian prison cell? What activates an earthquake so much so that it opens prison doors, yet records no physical damage to surrounding properties? What seismic event can, with laser beam accuracy, do what this one did? I heard a friend once say, "We do not play an instrument; we are in fact *the* instrument that brings praise, glory and honor to the King of Kings and the Lord of Lords.

There is no question of whether or not we should praise Him. This is a statement that declares, "He must be praised." The world needs a demonstration of the power of God. Amidst the mercy drops from place to place, and a minority of true Bible preachers, there is a spiritual bankruptcy in most pulpits, and, equally as alarming, there is flagrant sin in most music ministries. We are desperate for a revival of righteousness and a purging of sin, in order for God to show Himself to us. We must make Him welcome again, put out the red carpet and invite the Presence of God to our churches. I am not advocating for the worship of worship, but rather for the invitation that opens the door for God to move, miracles to happen, and mountains to tremble at His presence.

Long gone are the ones who once refused to be tainted with sin. Few and far between are those who truly minister for God, and God alone. You will be hard-pressed to find anyone who believes that a laborer is worthy of his hire more than me, yet we must not pursue paid performers hired only for their talent, rather than because they also walk in a Judah anointing. The subtle desensitization of our young people, who walk into the trap of the enemy, lured by success and fame, is the sad portrayal of many today. We must refuse to bow down to these idols of man that, having a form of godliness but no real power, are void of demonstration and are running on empty on the gauge of holiness. Our once filled altars for many have become "mosh pits" of idol worship and flesh-filled demonstrations of a generation that has forgotten God or replaced Him with a counterfeit.

Our ministry has possibly one of the most incredible teams of musicians and singers I have seen in almost 40 years of full-time ministry, and please forgive me if I sound boastful, but I must bring forth this understanding. Our team is loud and energetic, with screaming guitars and drummers who have to wear sweatbands on their foreheads so their vision is not impaired by the sweat dripping into their eyes. It includes keyboard players who do not only rely on 88 keys but add a second tier of keys, and singers who know, before they step onto the platform, that stilettos and high-heeled shoes just will not cut it when the Holy Ghost comes upon them. Nikes have become the footwear of choice and the control team needs a Red Bull, both before and after service, just to keep up. Our musicians do not get a paycheck and have never asked for one. Our singers are not staged, nor are they recruited from America's Got Talent or The Voice. Each one is not only hand-picked, but also prayed in. They are required to live holy and upright in their walk with God. They understand the importance of their position, and they are so well acquainted with the fear of God that they know that to step onto our platform with a life that is tainted by sin would risk them being struck by lightning. Far from perfect, but living in a state of continual perfection, each one seeks to bring glory to God through their voices and their instrumental talents.

Have our Church music programs become such a priority that we would dare to compromise? In our humble beginning, we started with an acoustic guitar and a stool. Anything that we have today, which would be the desire of most pastors across America, is only because we refused to allow something unholy into such a holy atmosphere. We were faithful with the little and God has blessed us with much. The anointing is not initiated by a band; it is given by God and flows through the pipeline of holiness, integrity, and credibility.

Judah does not need anything at all to operate, thus any of the peripheral additions that make up our times of praise and worship are beneficial, but not necessary for God to move. Pastors, if your music ministry cannot function in the absence of electricity, then what are you really dependent on? Do not wait to have everything lined up in your favor, or for the conditions to be just perfect. They already are. Judah has been here all along, ready and waiting to move through you.

Leah had three sons before Judah was born. Was she dealing with issues of rejection, of not being the first choice? Was she feeling the pain of inferiority, being fertile but forgotten? Many times, people miss opportunities, because their lives are shrouded in problems. While Judah waits, he is listening for the call and cry of a "Leah," a desperate, hurting person who finally resolves, after much of life has passed by, to respond to the opportunity to break the curse and sing.

Paul and Silas sat there, not only in the blackness of the midnight hour, but in the darkness of their dilemma. Everything possible had been done to them to prevent their escape. Their feet and hands were bound; their bodies were beaten; and their confinement was seemingly inescapable. To most, that would be the quitting factor. Who today would even survive to this point? I am sure such torture and pain would be avoided at all costs. Yet, they never considered saying, "Can we pay our way out of this?" or "We promise to never cast out a devil again if you will just let us go." Could they have apologized for preaching the Gospel with truth and passion, and without compromise and begged not to be thrown into the deepest part of the prison? Where are the Paul's and Silas' who, in this generation, are not afraid to ***"Let Judah Rise"*** and declare victory in the House of the Lord.

Isaiah 54 speaks of the barren woman whose womb was plagued with the inability to produce what should have been natural. You can imagine her cry increased, like the cry of many others desperately longing for a child, as she yearned to multiply, to increase, and to see her own offspring. Yet, even in barrenness, Isaiah encouraged her to sing. A Judah praise will bring forth miracles far beyond what you are humanly capable of doing. When you choose to sing, even from a position of pain, you release something into the atmosphere that brings expansion beyond that of a natural child. God will do even more than you can hope for or imagine. He will cause your seed, through your praise, to inhabit new territory and to make desolate cities to be occupied once again.

Barren churches are coming back to life again. Barren pulpits are getting ready to declare a fresh word of revival to the ears of desperate believers. The fallow ground is about to be broken up; the rain of Heaven is about to fall again, and as promised by God, this great "latter rain" will mesh with the "former rain" and the promised outpouring by the Prophet Joel will be upon us. ***"Let Judah Rise"***

CHAPTER ELEVEN

If Only You Had Been Here

Then said Martha unto Jesus, Lord, if Thou hadst been here, my brother had not died.

John 11:21

One of God's greatest gifts to us, other than Jesus Christ, is the wisdom of God. The Bible says, **"If any man lacks wisdom, let him ask of God"** (James 1:5). If we are truly called to be wise as serpents and harmless as doves, should we ever find ourselves a step or two behind what the enemy is doing? Should we not, as Christians, be well ahead of the enemy, blazing the trail long before he even gets going. The tragedy of many is that they find themselves in a position of "too little, too late," and in the world of "if only I had." Everyone has those moments, the "if only" moments in our lives, where we could have, should have, and possibly would have *if only* we could turn back time. But we cannot, and so we set our compass for the future and look to Jesus for direction.

Billy Graham once said, "Although I have much to be grateful for as I look back over my life, I also have many regrets. I have failed many times, and I would do many things differently. For one thing, I would speak less and study more, and I would spend more time with my family." Regret is a missed opportunity, something that has passed our life with no apparent ability to be recovered. The exception to every rule of man is God. What we call a regret, God may call an opportunity. What we perceive as the end, God may say, is only the beginning. We declare things over and finished and rule out the God factor. How many times do we find ourselves guilty of declaring the end of a thing when we are only in the second chapter of an eleven-chapter book? A deeper study into the attributes of God will help to quicken your faith to realize that believers have no right to declare the end of a thing, until God says it is over. Stop quoting the cliche phrases about God being the Alpha and the Omega, unless you truly believe that He is the Omega. We are often guilty of declaring memorized quotes but find ourselves in the shallow end of the pool of faith.

In the year 1948 a young watchmaker by the name of Louis Brandt, just 23 years of age, began a company, from his small workshop in a Swiss village, that would later become known as Omega. He eventually turned the business over to his sons, and their entire company was based upon creating the ultimate accomplishment and the final word in the watch industry. Today, the Omega watch is a global standard in the watch industry, and each watch is still built as if it can be outdone by no other.

When we ascribe to God the attribute of omniscience, we are declaring that he alone has the power to know the end from the beginning. When we consider the story of Lazarus, especially when we can, for just a moment, put ourselves in the position of his sister Martha, we see the frustration that must have been within her that day. She thought to herself, "If only He would have come on time. Why would He delay his arrival? Did He not know that whatever my brother had was going to kill him?" Martha was not a whole lot unlike most Christians today. Many believe and would be offended if their faith in God was questioned, suggesting that it was more like Martha's then they think. Of course Martha believed, but only up until the point of death. Death seems to be that final closing door, where our faith now settles into acceptance of the situation.

Just a couple years ago the strangest thing took place in our ministry. A man, whom I had heard about but never really knew, showed up in one of our services. It was unusual for several reasons, first because he lived almost six hours away and second, because, if you knew him, you would wonder what would make him come to a place where he had no family, no history, and no connections whatsoever. You see, this man had traveled the world, had seen great success in all his business ventures and, if measured by worldly standards, had it all. By this time, he was in his mid-fifties, still going strong and showing no signs of slowing down. So, what could possibly bring him our way?

Service after service he came in, extremely flamboyant, three thousand dollar shoes, Rolex watches, and exotic cars. He certainly made a statement, and anyone who could see him would quickly turn to watch him make his way to his seat. It was not his intention to draw attention to himself; it was just who he was. His position in life had, for many years, put him in the circle of high rollers, celebrities, Vegas personalities and people whose names many readers would recognize. His lifestyle of private jets, multi-million-dollar homes and extravagance was quite impressive to the world, I am sure. I was told he had made over two hundred and twenty million dollars in his life, but his story does not end there.

Little did I know that he would spend the last year of his life with us and our ministry. It was a mystery for a while, but the picture became much clearer in time. Even though his life had been one of wealth and opulence, it had taken a toll on his physical body. I came home from preaching our Sunday services to receive a phone call letting me know that he had died in the hospital. This came as quite a shock because although I knew he had some health issues, I was not expecting this.

It had only been just moments since, there in the hospital bed, he had stopped breathing. His sister called me crying, while sitting beside him, and said, "He's gone." I immediately told her to put the telephone to his ear and I began to pray. You see, it is not my job to heal, it is only my job to believe for God to heal. I began to speak life into his lifeless body and call him back from death. For several minutes I prayed over him but finally resolved that this was God's time to bring him home. I did know, with absolute certainty, that he made it to Heaven, and that was the greatest joy.

It was not long after he had passed away that his life story began to be told to me. You see, the reason God brought him to our ministry was to prepare him for eternity. He started out on the right path but got lost along the way. Had he died in that state, he most certainly would have gone to hell. God knew! The Omega of our lives knows all things, and He knew. When you know all things, urgency is not a part of your life. A preacher friend of mine once said, "Has it ever occurred to you that nothing ever occurs to God?"

His life was on a collision course for a Christless eternity; he was on his way to hell. God, the Omega, placed him into the arms of our ministry for the final year of his life, and in that year, all the crooked paths were made straight, all the years of running had come to an end, and today he is with Jesus.

"Oh Martha!" Jesus said, "Don't you know that your brother will rise again?" This is such a great story in the Bible about Lazarus being raised from the dead, but an equally great truth is found within the same chapter.

One of the most powerful revelations God gave me, when He put the words "Judah Rise" in my spirit, was that even though faith would be scarce in the last days, a remnant would arise, who would know a level of faith that goes beyond believing in God and rises to a level where miracles become common, everyday life occurrences. Judah rising is about Martha's faith moving to a new understanding. Martha believed, but only to the point of death, whereas this rising remnant of faith-filled people will see beyond the grave into situations where what man calls dead, God calls sleeping and He will awaken those that sleep.

The Church is alive, the Church is full of power, but within its walls are Marthas who fail to see the Omega of the Church displayed in all His glory and power. Let me take you to the even more incredible part of this story, where Judah is displayed. It was only days before the Passover feast. Lazarus was still alive, and together with Jesus, Mary and Martha, found himself in the house of Simon the Leper. As was the custom of that day, a gift was brought to the host of the dinner and the host reciprocated by washing the feet of his guests. This dinner was certainly not following protocol, when Mary chose to bypass the host to make her way to Jesus and there, lying at His feet, she broke open what cost her much. In her hands she held what would have cost the average person a year's wages, possibly her dowry for an upcoming wedding day, a box of very precious ointment, what we refer to as "the alabaster box."

With her hands stretched out, she poured it upon His feet and dried them with her hair, the symbol of a woman's glory. What an act of worship, a deep passionate cry for the one she loved the most. Estimated to be about twelve ounces of pure ointment, the fragrance filled the room.

Most of what is purchased today at perfume counters is a watered down, diluted semblance of the true fragrance it should be, and nowhere close to the purity of the fragrance Mary gave. David said these words, "How can I offer God something that cost me nothing?" What are we giving God today in our Houses of Worship? What did it cost us? We come into our church buildings, often with the same disposition of heart with which we would walk into a local department store. The desperate cry of expectation is a rarity in many, not to mention what we bring in with us. The majority of church attenders balk at having to give God ten cents on every dollar, when Mary gave everything she had. We need to be aware of the difference. A true Judah would never come into God's presence that way. Imagine saying to Jesus, "You are late. Where were you? If only you had been here," not even knowing that you are talking to the very One who can call dead things back to life again.

We find ourselves standing and weeping over what we feel we have lost, rather than rejoicing over what we are yet to gain. We have lost nothing if we have not lost Christ! We have the whole world to gain, with access to the unlimited possibilities God has made available to us, if we just learn to worship like Mary did.

We are living in a day where mainline denominations are now deliberating in back boardrooms over questions that would have once been considered unfathomable. As a young preacher, I vividly recall sitting in a general conference where a statement was made that drew the air from the lungs of all its hearers. In utter shock, we heard these words, "If we do not change course now, we will be ordaining homosexuals in 20 years." It seemed so far out there, that it caused many to wonder if this individual was in his right mind. That could never happen; the standards are too high; the Bible is too clear, and the movement is too secure to ever allow that to happen. Yet almost to the day, approvals came out of the boardrooms of apostate degenerate denominations, who not only deliberated, but actually gave approval for such a thing to happen. Today, the once behind closed doors lifestyle of the LGBTQ+ community now proudly flaunts itself not only in gay pride parades, but in the pulpits of our mainline denominational churches.

Of greater concern still is not just the liberal indoctrination in our once great colleges and universities in America, but on the campuses of many of what we once called Bible colleges. God, give us a revival on our college and university campuses. Fewer and fewer dot the landscape of our nation, and those that do, with the exception of just a few, have transitioned into what we have conveniently called "Liberal Arts." I do not even find that terminology in the Bible. What is "liberal" and what is "arts?" Ask our professors about the baptism in the Holy Spirit, ask them about the evidence of speaking in other tongues, ask them about their perspective on same sex marriage, and so forth, and be ready to ask for a chair if you are standing, because you will need it.

There is a reason why such liberalism has now taken root in many of our denominations. It is because they are no longer filled with the Spirit. Wherever there is an absence of God's Holy Spirit, there will be a thirst for the counterfeit. Have many become so open-minded that their brains fell out, and common sense, let alone divine wisdom, are both absent? We have conveniently named our churches in such a way that you have to be present in a service to try to determine what it believes, but once inside, many drink the Kool-Aid of a great song, a nice message, but no signs, no wonders, and certainly no miracles. Yes, there is a recent growth trend in evangelical churches, but the Church should not be identified by its productions or presentations. It should be identified by what is confirmed through the preaching of the Word of God.

Martha, you are a good woman, but you are found wanting. You have been found in a dangerous place of believing, but not recognizing Who it is that stands before you. Follow the example of your sister, run to the feet of Jesus, break open that precious act of worship before Him and ***"Let Judah Rise."***

CHAPTER TWELVE

Will He Find Faith On The Earth

I tell you that He will avenge them speedily. Nevertheless when the Son of man cometh, shall He find faith on the earth?

Luke 18:8

I did not watch the broadcast, but I do remember all the hype that surrounded the opening of Al Capone's vault. It was a two-hour live broadcast, hosted by none other than Geraldo Rivera, that focused entirely on the walled-off section of an underground room at the Lexington Hotel in Chicago. Thirty million people watched this highly rated, low impact special that, in the end, revealed nothing but dust and cobwebs. What caused it to draw the attention that it did? Was it the mystery surrounding the Capone era? I think people by nature are inquisitive, wanting to uncover unknown things.

One of the questions Jesus asked, in Luke 18:8, also causes us to wonder what the answer might be when the time comes: ***"When the Son of Man returns, will He find faith on the earth?"*** I have no doubt that there will be a remnant filled with great faith, but like the opening of Capone's vault, I am sure there will be a plethora of empty, dusty, cobweb-filled lives with nothing of substance inside. What were once vaults filled with mountain-moving faith may very well become the almost prophetic fulfillment of the question Jesus asked, "Will I find faith on the earth?"

We are warned to never take away or add anything to the Word of God, so I am cautious about doing that, and never would, unlike some versions of the Bible; but it is possible, I believe, to bring clarification to this question regarding the finding of faith. If for clarity I could invert it, I would say, "He will find faith on the earth." The question not being, will He, but how much? Will faith at the time of the coming of the Lord be rarer than a Pittsburgh steak? It is important because faith is the foundation upon which the Christian Church is built. It is your foundation and without it, what hope do we have?

In Galatians 6:9, Paul talks about the effect of leaven. Leaven is a form of yeast, which is most often used to make bread rise. On one hand, Paul is speaking about the effect of leaven in the life of a Christian and how, if not guarded, we can allow such a small thing to affect our entire life. Sin has this effect, and for this reason, we are to avoid the very appearance of evil, which is something that needs to be preached often in our pulpits today. Leaven can be an improper glance, a wrong motive, a bitter spirit left unchecked, or it can be something as simple as not putting back the shopping cart at the grocery store. Leaven in this biblical sense is deceiving. It is when we think it will not affect us, and thus leave it untouched, that we will, over time, see its effects, much like bread dough left to rise on the counter a little too long. Leaven can be the deception of justification, the convincing of oneself that we are okay in what we are doing. How many times have I heard, "We are married in the eyes of God?" I am afraid that this is one of the effects of the conditioning influence of sin. Do not blame God for your unwillingness to do things the right way, or your weakness of the flesh, or your rebellion against God's Word. This is the very thing that weakens the Church and discredits Christianity in the eyes of the world. Quit justifying sin! At what point did you allow a little leaven into your life? Where did the enemy get his foot in the door of your heart, only to bring you to the place you are today?

It was September 2, 1984, when flight 007 was shot down in Soviet airspace with 269 passengers on board. A computer malfunction resulted in a small navigational error that, though unnoticeable in the beginning, caused the massive 747 aircraft to stray off course over time. Imagine so many lives lost because of a minute navigational error. This is how leaven works. A seemingly tiny, almost imperceptible error in the beginning, to which we pay no mind, ends up having a disastrous effect on our relationship with God, and ultimately on our lives. Ephesians 4:27 tells us to, ***"Neither give place to the devil."*** Give him no room, no place in your life!

Growing up, we lived in the north part of the city of Toronto Canada, and though it was relatively safe, we locked our doors. I remember if I ever got locked out of the house, which happened often especially on the coldest of winter days, that I had a backup plan. I had a window leading to the basement that I knew, if I pushed in the right spot, would allow me to get in the house. Any opportunity for the devil to get in is what he is looking for in our lives. Locked doors, and windows in my case, are a deterrent to the devil. Closed doors are good, locked doors are better, but open doors are dangerous ground.

The enemy is so intent on your destruction that he will wait like a lion in the grass for as long as necessary to see if you will drop your guard. His nature is tenacious, so much so that his determination to attack you can be greater than your strength to withstand him. He is a deceiver, who uses the leaven approach to convince you that a little dabbling in sin, here and there, will not hurt you. But it will. It might even destroy you!

If God questions the presence of faith upon the earth when He returns, what would be the things that lead to its demise in some people? It always begins subtly, with nothing harsh, nothing abrupt, but rather with a slow turn in the wrong direction. Of greater concern is that the real picture of this tragic decline of faith will be in the faithless people who are still standing in our churches on Sundays, feigning worship. Often, a faith struggle stems from a situation or conflict between two brothers or sisters in the Church, a transaction gone wrong, hurt feelings, or a bad business deal. Any one of those can take people who are not strong in their faith into a downward spiritual spiral. Other things that can deflate your faith are ungodly soul connections, such as when you are with the wrong people or with the wrong crowd. When you hang around unspiritual people, everything will become unspiritual. We are called to win them, not fellowship with them. God said, "***What fellowship hath light with darkness?***".(II Corinthians 6:15)

Other areas we must guard ourselves against are in the realm of excessive grief and mourning. These are often access points for the enemy to invade our lives, especially our thought life, which can ultimately affect our faith. Remember, we are talking about God finding faith when He returns. Only you can ask yourself this question, do you have faith?

Let us come back to the title of this book for just a moment, "Judah Rise!" I graduated from Bible College in 1985. The denomination I was a part of at the time was not happy with me attending a Bible College, as that was not within their denominational framework. So, I suppose I had already started out with them on the wrong foot. But I remember specifically praying, "God, if I am going to preach the Gospel like you have called me to do, I need to go where You will best prepare me to do it." Who can argue with that? Well, the denomination did not see it my way, and ultimately, I ended up departing from that particular sect. I know that God can move both within the denominational framework and outside of it. He is not limited in any way, but I must say, there was a much greater liberty, once I left, than I ever felt within it. Maybe it was the fact that they did not like my school choice, but since then, most of their Bible schools have either closed or turned into something else; so, all in all, I made the right choice, as my Bible School is still going strong today.

While in Bible College, I learned things that had not been taught to me growing up in the Pentecostal Church I attended. Interestingly, the Pentecostal heritage goes back many generations in my family line, and some of my predecessors were instrumental in bringing the Gospel and starting Bible Colleges in Tanzania and Kenya. Other relatives have authored many books still used today. As a Pentecostal preacher by experience, I grew up hearing the basic fundamentals of

Pentecost but rarely ever saw a demonstration. I soon realized that there was more, and that the purpose of preaching the Gospel was not only to see men saved, but also set free, healed, and delivered.

Miracles were seldom seen or even talked about, and in an era not long after, great healing tent revivals were taking place all over the United States. I could not help but be prompted to desperately want more of God. What I did learn, more by experience than by textbooks and Bible School classes, was the reality of the miraculous through faith. I learned that faith can move mountains, and that when I pray, believing and expecting to receive, I can have whatever I desire. What I learned has never left me, and, in fact, it has kept me in a perpetual state of revival since my youth.

Your faith must be growing for it to be working! Faith must be fed continually with the Word of God, which expands our capacity to believe for greater things. I believe it was Dr. Lester Sumrall who said that we are to, "Feed our faith and starve our doubts and fears to death." A law in our universe states that nothing ever remains the same, and that change is constant; and likewise, our faith should be in a continual state of expansion, while always remaining grounded in the Word.

Newton, in his second law of thermodynamics, said that "Anything left on its own over a period of time will eventually deteriorate." This is the very reason why, moment by moment, hour by hour, our faith must be stirred up. To stir something up means to wake it up or cause it to *rise up*. Many once great men and women of God have allowed their faith to grow weary, no longer living in that place of believing in miracles daily. This spiritual state is to be avoided at all costs, and the only way to do that is to stir our faith up.

"Judah Rise" is a call to the Church, and to every believer, to refuse to allow our lives to slide down the slippery slope of gradualism into the pool of apathy. It is a clarion call to those who know what to do but are not doing it. "Judah Rise" is a sound from Heaven calling the troops to get back into their battle fatigues and prepare themselves for war. The Captain of the Hosts, the Lord Jesus Himself is calling. Heaven is calling and we stand at this pivotal moment, between our history and our future, in our fight for the Kingdom.

Several years ago, our youngest daughter and I were rushing to get to the airport. I had just finished preaching a Sunday service and was meeting the rest of the family for vacation. They had decided to leave a few days earlier, and so I stayed behind with our youngest and would fly out after preaching. By this time in ministry, I had preached hundreds of messages on faith, declared it from pulpits around the world, laid hands on untold thousands for healing and deliverance, built churches, Christian Schools and much more. Faith was my thing, and by that I mean it is what came out of me everywhere I went; but to be honest, in almost all cases, it was faith for someone else, for their need or miracle.

If there was someone with a need, I would have them at the altars, covered in oil, hands laid on their heads, as I declared supernatural intervention in Jesus' name. So, now we found ourselves on our way to the airport, about an hour's ride away. I felt myself growing frustrated because our driver was slow, and because I am a calculated person, I had already measured time over distance and had come to the conclusion that, if we did not go any faster, we would not make the flight. My little daughter Madison was looking up at me, excited to get with the rest of the family and looking forward to a much-needed family vacation together. As she looked to me for reassurance, I quietly turned to her and whispered, “Honey, we might not make this flight, but don’t worry, there’s lots of other planes.” Although she was only about 8 years old at the time, she was sharp and quick to respond, “No daddy, we will make it.”

Being the world traveler that I was, and of course so much smarter than her, I smiled and patted her on the head as if to say, “Okay, we’ll see.” I had traveled this road a thousand times; I knew the traffic patterns and was well aware that we still had a border crossing to go through, not to mention that we were dealing with a driver that did not know a car could go over forty five 45 miles an hour. Our flight departed at 3 pm and we were still an hour away, with only 15 minutes left before departure. I turned to Madison again and said, “Honey, I’m really sorry. I will get us a nice hotel, and we will get on another airplane tomorrow.”

Immediately, she again affirmed, “No daddy, we will make it!” By now I just left it alone, as I was not going to go back and forth with an eight-year-old on her first flight. I mean, how credible could an eight-year-old child, who did not drive yet and barely even knew how to tell time, be? It was 3 pm, the flight had already boarded, and we were just crossing the border, still at least fifteen minutes from the airport. By this time, I was telling the driver, "Don't even bother rushing; the flight has gone."

With each passing moment, my faith was decreasing, because my confession was negative. I had already based my faith on printed pieces of paper and made the decision without even consulting God as to whether or not we would make it. We arrived at the airport about twenty minutes after the scheduled departure time of the flight. By this point, I was just slowly gathering our luggage out of the trunk of the car and casually strolling into ticketing, with Madison pulling on my arm saying, "Come on daddy, let's go!" I have to admit that, at this juncture, I was just patronizing her, and began to make it look like I was rushing. I knew that we still had security to go through and that we could not even check our bags, because we were too late. Then, all of a sudden, I heard these words echo over the entire airport loudspeaker system, "Reverend Stephen Bilsborough and Miss Madison Bilsborough, this is the last call; we are holding the plane." I was shocked! We started running, Madison pulling her little Barbie suitcase, while I pulled mine, for what seemed like a mile, until we finally made it to the gate, down the ramp and onto the plane. We sat down, buckled our seatbelts, and as sweat started running down my cheeks, Madison turned to me and said, "See, daddy, I told you we would make it!"

Faith is not quantified by the number of degrees we have on our walls, nor by the years of experience we have. Faith is the very thing Jesus spoke about when He said we must become as a little child to enter into Heaven. Faith is not pushing the right buttons to manipulate a situation, nor is it saying the right words to entice people to give. Faith is simply believing that God can, and God will, perform what He has promised and then declaring it.

Will He find faith? That depends on whether we allow Judah to rise up within us. Will we, with confidence, know that when the battle rages, we call on Judah to go first? Will we praise, shout, and run into battle with the assurance that greater is He who is in us than He that is in the world. ***"Let Judah Rise"***

CHAPTER THIRTEEN

You Shall Have Dominion

And God said, Let us make man in our image, after our likeness: and let them have dominion over the fish of the sea, and over the fowl of the air, and over the cattle, and over all the earth, and over every creeping thing that creepeth upon the earth.

Genesis 1:26

The pattern was set by God in Genesis Chapter One. He put a system into order for man to live within and be blessed by. What it must have been like to live in the Paradise of Eden, with no sickness and no death, simply thriving in God's original plan! Can you imagine being given dominion over everything, with the exception of just one tree?

I have visited some pretty impressive botanical gardens in the places we have traveled, often looking at the creativity of God, in awe of His grand display of beauty. I can only imagine what the Garden of Eden must have been like. Described as unlike anything known to man, this is where God began all things, in the midst of perfection.

It was in the place called Eden that God gave dominion to man, to Adam, the first man, and to those who would come from him. God literally intended for man to rule the planet, having full authority over everything upon the face of the earth. Everything that God breathed into Adam was breathed into you. That same dominion and authority that God gave to him, He gave to you. To have authority over something puts you in a position where everything below you must listen to you. The voice of Adam in the Garden was enough to cause every living thing to listen and obey. This hierarchy of God, imparted to man, was God's pattern of how things were and of how they are still intended to be. It was bestowed to Adam and Eve, as a seed to be passed on from generation to generation, even to you today.

Why God chose to use the method of a seed is because a seed is designed by God to reproduce after its own kind. The seed of authority in man was not only designed to flow from generation to generation, but also to increase from generation to generation. This is why the devil is often referred to as the "seed eater," because he knows the power of the seed. The blessing is upon you, upon your children and upon your children's children, increasing with each generation. It is God's exponential supernatural growth.

God did not say to Adam, "You shall have defeat." He said, "You shall have dominion." Yet many believers today live in a position of defeat, and do not even realize it. If you listen to what comes out of their mouths, you can hear their downtrodden disposition in words like "I hope so" or "It sure would be nice." Faith dares to step out onto nothing and believe that God will sustain you. How can someone say, "God is good" in one breath and, in the next, say, "I don't know how I'm going to make it." The words, "I hope so" should almost be removed from the vocabulary of Christians. I am amazed when I pray for people at altars and ask the question, "Do you believe God will heal you today?" The response knocks me back each time, "Well, I hope so." What do you mean, you hope so? Faith calls those things that be not as though they are. Faith praises and thanks before the manifestation; it does not wait for it to happen. Many people today have been so infiltrated with bad teaching that their faith has fallen by the wayside.

The reason I call the devil the seed eater is because seventy five percent of every message preached is taken from Christians within fifteen minutes of walking out of the Church. Perched on the parking lot light posts are the enemies, birds of prey, devourers waiting to snatch whatever little faith you might have left, sending you into another week of dismal doubt and fainting faith. Jesus himself spoke of the parable of the sower, and how the seed of God's Word was the prized possession of the devil, doing whatever he could to stop it from taking root in the hearts of people. When we buy a new appliance, we read the manual; when we purchase a new car, we read the manual. Likewise, God gave us a manual, called the Bible, which works every single time we use it.

I was preaching one time in the country of Mozambique, in an AFM Church. They had a guest cabin for preachers, so following the service, that is where I stayed. The service went late, and it was the darkest night I have ever seen in Africa. As I made my way back to the place they had me staying, one of the ladies from the church who had just been powerfully touched by God, rode back with us. My driver, this lady and I made our way to the cabin, where, on the front porch, was a small metal can. I did not think anything of it, but the lady lunged back in fear. Her facial expression was unmistakably filled with horror, prompting me to ask her what was wrong. She said, “That’s a witch doctor’s spell. He has put a curse over you. You must not go in there.” I said, “Did God not just touch your life? Who is more powerful, a witch doctor or God?” I was astounded when, even at that, she hesitated to answer. I knew the only thing I could do to help this poor fear-filled woman was to show her; so, I took the can, which was filled with goat’s blood, and threw it into the forest and said, “In the name of Jesus I break every demonic curse off of this house, and I render every witch doctor powerless.” The problem with some Christians is that they cannot discern when it is time to think and when it is time to act. In this case, I did not need to stop and think about it, because had I done so, my senses would have kicked in, my soul would have begun to make suggestions to my subconscious, and I could possibly have begun to wonder if there really was any power in a witch doctor's curse. I simply acted, and God was honored by an "act of faith."

After a great night's rest, when I got up the next morning, the driver and that same lady were at the door waiting. I said, "How are you?" She said, "Wonderful! I am free from the fear of witch doctors forever, because you have shown me that God is more powerful than any witch doctor."

The same power that raised Jesus Christ from the dead, dwells in me. Stop to think for just a moment, how Jesus Himself told us in John 14:12 that greater works would we do. Why? Because He goes to His Father which is in Heaven. In Mark 16:19, the question of where Jesus went is answered: He is seated in dominion and authority at the right hand of the Father! All day long, He is seated, enforcing the original covenant with you and I. Every time the devil tries to challenge your authority, simply look up as if you were looking into the Gates of Heaven and be reminded that Jesus is sitting on the throne. The Bible tells us that right after Jesus was taken up into Heaven, His disciples traveled everywhere preaching, and Jesus confirmed His Word through them with signs following.

In other words, as long as we are following the pattern of God and are doing the work of God, Jesus will just keep confirming His Word. He is confirming salvations today, healings today, miracles today, breakthroughs today!

We have a habit of praying for people all the time, but when I pray for people at our altars, I always take authority over whatever is causing them a problem. If it is cancer, I take authority over cancer; if it is depression, I take authority over depression. Many people I pray for have what I call a "spirit of infirmity." In other words, they always have something wrong with them, which just follows them all the days of their lives; so I take authority over spirits of infirmity, and we continue to see many doctor-verified miracles.

Why must Judah go first, is because it is only in that order that these things happen. The God of order designed it this way. Judah must go first in order to ensure the victory. One of the Hebrew words for praise is Jehovah Nissi, the Lord our Banner. In Exodus 17, Moses built an altar and called the name of the place Jehovah Nissi, the Lord our Banner, declaring victory over Amalek. The banner of the Lord raised high declares the enemy defeated before the battle even begins.

It was Winston Churchill who inspired his soldiers during the most difficult days of battle to always see the victory before the battle begins. His motivating and masterful messages brought hope in Britain's darkest hours. Let our spiritual leaders of today be indomitable in retreat, invincible in advance, and insufferable in victory, as declared by Churchill to his Field Marshal Sir Bernard Montgomery.

We have, for far too long, failed to keep the tip of the sword in the face of the enemy. We have retreated, sometimes unaware, making way for the opposition to gain ground. We have never been called to make friends with the world; we are only called to win it. Why should we be bankrupt of discernment, while the Trojan horse from hell, filled with venomous vipers' intent on murdering the innocent and on injecting compromise and complacency through the syringe of political correctness and wokeism, slips past the gates of our churches and homes and into our children and families?

Judah must rise, and God's people must once again look up to see Moses's hands held high. We must see the horses and chariots of the Lord's army knowing that those that are with us, more than those that are against us. We must prepare to smash our lanterns, as in Gideon's battle, and put confusion in the camp of the enemy. Our methods must return to our roots, and we must understand that there is but one unchangeable paradigm, the power of the Holy Ghost in our lives, in our churches, in our homes and in our cities.

Dominion is not something that is just taught; it is already within us. But for some, it still lies unrecognized, untapped, and lying dormant, until such time as this sleeping giant is awakened. Like a blind man seeing for the very first time or a crippled person walking who has never walked before, so must be the posture of every believer upon the realization of the power that lies within. Yes, it will be met with resistance. You will have those who say you are extreme, and some may even refer to it as "hyper faith." But I would much rather err on the side of hyper faith than hesitant faith. I would rather believe God for too much and be wrong, then for too little and be right. The religious crowd will never embrace the supernatural because they sift it through their senses and analyze it until it is asphyxiated. People who discover new lands had no one to follow after. They blazed trails and carved new paths in uncharted territory. Today, we can hardly go to the grocery store without a GPS.

This is not a book about redefining our purpose or refining our programs; it is about reviving our purpose. What has been concealed in the cloud of confusion, in the haze of humanism, is coming to light. Judah is rising! Eyes are opening, and hearts are hearing and beating again with the life of Jesus, with the very same passion of the cross for a lost and dying world, that can only ever be changed by those who refuse to cower to the crowds.

God, give us men and women who will not bow before those standing in the balconies, who have been weighed in the balance and been found wanting. Give us those who have no need for acceptance and no fear of rejection, knowing that they have been given all that they need to fulfill the call.

If we have, even for a moment, ever thought that sin was intended to be the dominant force in this world, we are theologically misled. If sin has had any opportunity for dominance, it is only because of the shallow thinking of those who refused to embrace what God gave us in Genesis Chapter One. You shall have dominion! Dominion over cancer and COVID, dominion over plagues and paralysis, dominion over sickness and disease, dominion over everything. Sin caused man to lose his place in the garden, but the cross bought it all back. Let Judah Rise!

Billy Sunday, one of America's great outfielders in baseball was also considered one of the most influential evangelists during the early 1900's. Concerning sin, he said "I'll kick it as long as I've got a foot, I'll fight it as long as I've got a fist, I've butt it as long as I've got a head, and I'll bite it as long as I've got a tooth. And when I'm old, fistless, footless, and toothless, I'll gum it till I go home to glory, and it goes home to perdition."

Man has power over sin. The Blood of Jesus Christ forgave us, and the power of the Holy Spirit enables us to not only walk in freedom and victory over sin, but even more than that, to have dominion over all things.

I grew up in the snow. We lived in it four to five months of the year, for most of our lives. It was normal. As normal as a summer day was a bitter winter morning. We dressed for it, as we had all the proper attire, boots, mitts, hats, and scarves. The cold was inevitable, but what we did to counteract it was a choice. We can become a victim of something or defend against it. "Dress for the weather" is something we heard from our parents all of our growing up days. Sadly, many Christians do not properly prepare for what they will encounter, once outside the doors of our sanctuaries. A sanctuary is a place of refuge, safety, and protection, a place where, once inside, we have some degree of assurance that we will be okay; but beyond the walls, many have not adequately prepared themselves to stand against the wiles of the devil.

The bitter sting of sin has caused frostbite in many churches, so much so that, for most, there is a numerical and spiritual decline. Interest has faded because they have not seen a true demonstration in so very long. Instead, rather than faith, the world saw fear disguised as genuine concern for our brothers. Pastors stood in pulpits during COVID, declaring our necessity to care for our neighbors and to be considerate of others, saying all the things that would make their words more palatable to the lukewarm, and to the totally lost. Meanwhile, what they had really done is put their churches on palliative care, easing the symptoms without curing the underlying disease. The disease is sin, the answer is God, and the cure is the Word. Throughout the COVID pandemic, I prayerfully considered what God would have me to do. We have a large congregation and an extensive television audience, and I have a responsibility to navigate through difficult waters, leading those whom God has called me to lead.

As I prayed, God said, lead them as I would lead them, lead them in faith and not in fear. He also said, "I gave man the freedom of choice; you must do the same." I heard the Lord and preached two words throughout the pandemic, faith and freedom, faith to not be afraid and freedom to do what you want. We never stopped having one service throughout the entire ordeal. Every week, we continued to reach many thousands through live services, online broadcasts, and television broadcasts. People had choices: "Wear a mask or don't wear a mask, get a shot or don't get a shot." I left it up to each individual to make the choice and only encouraged them to make it after seeking the Lord's will with much prayer.

How can I stand as a preacher of the Gospel and allow fear to permeate hearts? God told me in Genesis 1:26 that I have dominion and authority over all manner of sickness and disease.

"And when he had called unto him his twelve disciples, he gave them power against unclean spirits, to cast them out and to heal all manner of sickness and all forms of disease" (Matthew 10:1).

Many people failed the test, although most will not want to admit it. But failing a test does not mean that you have been discounted; it simply means that come next time, you need to be ready. The world needs a Church that will be a true example of faith and authority, that will cause them to be like the crowds that followed Jesus. The crowds that followed Jesus, did not understand how He did what He did, they simply knew that wherever he went, people got healed. They followed Jesus because they saw the works that He did. The religious crowd followed Him, the press followed Him, the skeptics followed Him, all because they knew He was not like the others. People are looking for leaders to follow that do not have a gimmick or a trick. They want to follow the truth, even if they do not understand it all. They will follow because they know what is real and what is not.

The line is drawn in the sand, the wheat is separating from the chaff, and this Judah generation is rising up to not be like the others. The world seeks the supernatural, we have to let them see it. How can we preach a Christ who opened blind eyes, and yet not raise people up out of hospital beds, disconnecting them from ventilators and chemotherapy and wheelchairs? How can we preach a Christ who told his disciples to go and heal all manner of sickness and disease and then accept a Church void of the supernatural works of God?

It can start with one. It only takes one to rise up. It can start with you. If there is more, then this is your moment to run after it. God would never have called you Judah, if He did not also give you what you needed to defeat every enemy in your way. He is calling you up today, to be the first to go, the first to conquer, the first to win! ***"Let Judah Rise"***

CHAPTER FOURTEEN

No Room In Judah For Idols

And he did that which was right in the sight of the LORD, and walked in the ways of David his father, and declined neither to the right hand, nor to the left.

II Chronicles 34:2

You know that when the golf courses are full and the boat ramps are busy on Sundays, that we may be suffering from the same problems the Children of Israel had most of their Old Testament history, idols. Over time we have changed their shape and form and their size and color, but we still have them, despite the fact that they are the very things God hates the most. Idolatry is a learned lifestyle. Children today learn to idolize the things they see their parents pay attention to the most, but back in the Old Testament, Israel learned idolatry because that is the atmosphere in which they were immersed, while they were under Egyptian bondage. So, we can understand why, over a period of four hundred years, as one Israelite generation passed away and another came to be, idols became more a part of their lifestyle. That is why the wealth of Egypt was not the only thing the children of Israel carried away with them in the Exodus. They also carried the baggage of idolatry. When it comes to a relationship with God, He does not share. God is a jealous God, and He created man only for Himself.

I could not possibly talk about *Judah Rise* without also talking about one of the greatest moves of God in the southern Kingdom of Judah. Idol worship has been a part of human history as long as history has been recorded and is still very much alive today. We just have different looking idols. It is incredible to see the nation of Judah under the leadership of its youngest king ever. Josiah was only eight years old. I truly believe that this coming Judah generation will be marked by a great variety of people, but the younger generation is going to be mightily used by God. In Acts Chapter 12, it was a young damsel named Rhoda, whom God used as a messenger to bring the news that Peter was at the gate of the courtyard, and they called her insane for doing so. They all thought it could not be Peter, as he was in prison. But it was Peter, and God used

Rhoda to bring the message. Much of this coming move of God will be led by our children and youth.

Josiah was unique in that, when you would think he would have preferred many other things, he demonstrated a genuine hunger for God, but not just for himself, but for the entire southern Kingdom. The only thing that will bring revival is repentance. We make the mistake so often of bringing a mixture of things to the table, hoping that it will usher in a revival, but nothing can do that, only repentance. The first thing King Josiah did was move from personal repentance to calling the entire southern Kingdom to repent and rid the nation of idols. Because man was created by God, he was designed to worship something, and so in the absence of God, man will make a god of something else. It is only when man rids his life of idols, that he will turn to serve the true and living God.

I was preaching in Mumbai, India a few years back and in a crowd of ten to fifteen thousand people, I gave an altar call, to which thousands responded to give their lives to Jesus. As I was giving the altar call, one of the pastors on the platform told me to tell them to turn their back on all their other gods. He said that preachers came there all the time and gave altar calls but, although the people responded, many eventually went back to all the other gods, because they viewed our God as just one of many gods. When I prayed with the crowd of probably five to seven thousand people, I had them repeat the prayer of salvation and told them to say, "I renounce all other gods." It was like a freedom swept through that airport field that day, smashing spiritual idols and gods who were hindering them from coming to Jesus. When idols, the gods of man, are removed from our lives, then man will turn to serve the true and living God. This is what began to happen in Judah. The people destroyed the idols and began to turn to God.

During this time, the temple had fallen into disrepair, and so Josiah called the people to begin to repair the temple and restore it again as a House of Worship. While workmen were reconstructing the temple, they discovered the lost scrolls of the Law of Judah. How far had they fallen away from God that they did not even know that they were void of the Word? What an incredible story of restoration and of how God used a young boy to bring a nation back into alignment with Him.

When the House is in order, and the Word is exalted, and idolatry is abolished, you can be assured that revival is imminent. A covenant was made that day to restore everything back to God's original plan and because of that, Judah observed the greatest Passover feast they had since the time of Samuel.

For revival to come, idols must go. Judah must rise above every other thing in our lives. Notice this young king refused to walk to the right or to the left. The up-and-coming generation will be a generation who refuses to touch what is not holy. It will be a bold generation, a blessed generation, that will experience the strongest anointing upon their lives. These Judah's will refuse to be called the son of Pharaoh's daughter, choosing rather to endure the scorching heat of adversity, than to be numbered among the masses perishing in a Christless eternity.

Send Judah first! Is this generation of young people, who seem like they are surgically attached to their cell phones, almost as if they were incapable of being detached from them, who at times show little to no interest in the things of God, the generation that God is going to use? Are these the ones that, if ignited with the fervent kerosene of Heaven, will run up the hill to battle, shouting the praises of our God? Will this be the generation that, when seeing no place of victory, will inquire of the Lord and follow His leading, and listen to His voice, bringing confusion to the camp of the enemy? Will they be the David's, the Gideons, the Josiah's of their generation?

If we have been weakened in any way, it is the kryptonite of idolatry that has lured this generation into a lifestyle that embraces some of the world and some of God. But God does not share Himself, and He never will. This strange mixture will not survive this Judah generation. They will rise up and be free of what once attracted them and take on a new form. This, I believe, will be the generation Joel prophesied about, in which young men and young women will prophecy. If a Josiah can lead a nation into repentance, imagine what this generation can do. Imagine a young person touched by the fire of God, ignited, equipped, and trained to be one of this great army of Judah warriors.

Let Judah Rise and run to the front lines of the battle, with victory assured. Let the Church refuse to live an inert lifestyle, void of power and demonstration. Let families be restored and fathers be reunited with God. Let the Holy Spirit be the most welcome guest in our lives and in our churches. Where we have replaced Him with music with no anointing and preaching with no power, let Judah Rise again and fill our hearts for you God. May our pursuit be relentless, our passion be unquenchable and live our lives until our King returns, always putting the ***"Kingdom First."***